D0202145

THE HI-LINE

PROFILES OF A MONTANA LAND

Text and Photographs by
Daniel N. Vichorek

Montana Magazine
American & World Geographic Publishing

Vichorek, Daniel N.
     The Hi-line : profiles of a Montana land : text and photo-
graphs / by Daniel N. Vichorek.
          p.   cm.
     Includes bibliographical references and index.
     ISBN 1-56037-021-1
     1. Hi-Line (Mont. : Region)--History.   2. Hi-Line (Mont. :
Region)--Geography.   I. Title.
     F737.H55V53   1993
     978.6--dc20   92-44021

Printed in U.S.A.

ACKNOWLEDGMENTS

First, I would like to thank all the people named in this book who gave up some of their valuable time to talk to an itinerant reporter. Special thanks to Connie Huso and his friends in Kevin who put me straight on oilfield lingo, taught me the difference between a roustabout and a roughneck, and much more. I am particularly indebted to them for providing the taped interview with Charlie Stalnaker.

Thanks to Stacy Braaten in the Corps of Engineers office in Fort Peck, who got stuck handling photos for me, and without whom I wouldn't have had same. Thanks as usual to Dave Walter, reference librarian at the State Historical Society, who provided many a quaint and curious volume of obscure and ancient lore.

And of course, my gratitude to Lory Morrow and Becca Kohl, photo archivists extraordinaire at the Historical Society. And to the folks at the state library, who didn't send the cops when I kept the books too long.

I am thankful to Ron Harmon at Big Bud, who reviewed my first draft regarding his tractors.

For their special assistance, my thanks to the Bowlers of Scobey, to Doris Vallard in Glasgow, and—last but not least—a tip of the fedora to Doug Plouffe at the Sleeping Buffalo.

CONTENTS

MONTANA'S HI-LINE

There actually are people living in Montana who don't know what the Hi-Line is, where it is, or even how to spell it. Sometimes it is Highline, High Line, or Hi Line. Roberta Carkeek Cheney, in her book *Names on the Face of Montana,* wrote that the term "High Line" refers both to the route of Highway 2 and to the route of the Great Northern Railway, now the Burlington Northern.

Ms. Cheney's definition of the Hi-Line says it "extends roughly from Poplar…ending up in Glacier National Park." Gary A. Wilson in his book, *Honky Tonk Town: Havre's Bootlegging Days,* wrote that the term originally referred to the position of the Great Northern Railway as the northernmost railroad in the state. Wilson defines the Hi-Line as extending along the rails and Highway 2 from North Dakota to the Continental Divide. This is the definition I have chosen to adopt here.

Some people east of Poplar do not generally think of their territory as part of the Hi-Line, even though Highway 2 and the BN tracks continue east through that remote real estate. If the mental territory known as the Hi-Line ends at Poplar, it may reflect only a failure of the imagination. In the western part of the state, a lot of people get scared when they think of the country past Wolf Point, or even Havre. They are like the Portuguese sailors five and a half centuries ago trying to sail around the tip of Africa for the first time. They knew that beyond some point, there were bound to be monsters, if not the actual edge of the world.

The idea of being away from mountains, trees, and clear running streams is appalling to the tree- and mountain-bound people of the West, sometimes referred to as the "knapweed and condominium crowd." Similarly, a lot of people brought up on the Hi-Line don't have any fondness for mountains and trees. These obstructions obscure the view, probably interfere with the weather, and seem to defy gravity. Hi-Liners get uneasy when there is something higher than they are, and have the feeling such objects may fall on them at any moment. Some Hi-Liners may stray over to the Flathead during the hot season, but no doubt they are glad to get back home again afterward.

A militant Glasgow lad with two or three beers aboard sought to educate me in these matters. "The Big Sky ends at Browning, you know," he said, ready to fight for this sentiment. "There's no Big Sky in those mountains. They should call it the Tiny Sky Country over there." So there.

Some things about the Hi-Line suggest a certain uniformity. Just a few hundred yards from the reconstructed old Fort Union trading post on the Missouri, the Burlington Northern Railroad comes over flat land into Montana. Hundreds of miles to the west, past Browning, it leaves the flat land and enters the other world of the Rocky Mountains. Movie stars. Swimming pools. Knapweed. In between these eastern and western crossings, the rails run shiny and straight through a host of communities. These range from the disappearingly small to the comparable metropolises such as Wolf Point, Glasgow, Havre, Shelby, and Cut Bank. Each town, large and small, has at least one grain elevator by the tracks, a monument to grain, another of the universals of the Hi-Line life.

Besides the grain, there is oil, natural gas, livestock, even mining, and each of these has had its exhilarating booms and catastrophic busts. These days, one of the most promising sights on the Hi-Line is the migrant Canadian with his pockets full of money, hungry for cheap goods and entertainment. Each town has its thinkers trying to figure out how to harvest more of this Canadian cash.

Tourists pass through the Hi-Line country by the thousands, but show a strong disinclination to stop for anything other than gas. Research indicates that over 200,000 cars pass Wolf Point on Highway 2 each year, for example, many of them on their way to or from Glacier Park. Despite this potential bonanza of tourist dollars, there are no bona fide tourist traps along the Hi-Line, unless you count modest homegrown attractions such as the Sleeping Buffalo Resort near Saco, and the reconstructed "Havre Beneath the Streets." Although these developments would appeal to some tourists, they are not in the same league with western shrines such as Wall Drug, the Reptile Gardens, or even Gil's Gift Shop.

As shown in the table on page 122, population on the Hi-Line has been shrinking for several decades. Small farms have gotten bigger and more mechanized, more kids have grown up and sought the bright lights. Some Hi-Liners see virtue in the loss of population, citing the shake-out of inefficient farmers and their replacement by better ones. Others note that many Hi-Liners who have gone elsewhere to make a living would gladly return if there were economic opportunity for them.

Many on the Hi-Line experience a pervasive anxiety that their small-town way of life is disappearing. News that a store is folding in any Hi-Line town moves rapidly across the region and inspires grimness throughout.

Space and great flat distances are common denominators on the Hi-Line, and small variations have big consequences. Merchants and other townsmen, say east of Malta, note unhappily that local citizens are willing to travel clear to Williston, North Dakota to shop at a Wal-Mart. Hi-Line towns, when considering their assets, place value on being located too far from bigger towns for local people to drive to shop. Malta is too far from Billings and Great Falls for casual shopping trips, Chinook is not, and this makes a difference. Most citizens are patriotic and would like to shop locally no doubt, but there are many reasons not to. There is, for example, the need to get away once in a while.

There are many balancing acts. Glasgow, pondering the possibility that Boeing may bring a good number of high-paid employees to its holdings on the former Glasgow Air Force Base, wonders if the new money will enrich the present businesses, or if it will be enough to bring a Wal-Mart, which might knock off the old downtown business district. In Shelby, a large Pamida store built for Canadian trade has brought more people into town and improved business.

One thing for sure, people who live on the Hi-Line are survivors. These are not your migrant Americans who follow jobs or rumors of jobs from state to state and generic town to generic town. They know where they belong, and most of them have demonstrated that they and their descendants will persist there tooth and nail until, perhaps, the end of creation. In short, perhaps unlike most people these days, they have a home.

GREAT NORTHERN RAILWAY

The Amtrak passenger train that crosses northern Montana every day is called the *Empire Builder*. The route itself is referred to as "The Route of the *Empire Builder*." This refers both to the train and to the man who built the railroad, James J. Hill. Upon his retirement in 1912, Hill said, "Most men who have really lived have had their great adventure. This railway is mine."

Hill was not your typical cannibalistic capitalist pirate-tycoon of the late 19th century. He was born in Ontario, and as a boy he first wanted to be a surgeon. This ambition was frustrated when he lost the sight in one eye. He then decided to become a sea captain, and he left home at age 18 to ship out for the Orient as a sailor. On his way to the ocean, he got stranded in St. Paul, Minnesota, where he found work as a clerk for a Mississippi River steamboat line, which at the time was a free-for-all dog-eat-dog business.

He must have liked the work because he kept at it for nine years, educating himself on the side in everything from steamboat operations to history and law. Presently he went into business for himself, and the rest of the story could have been written by Horatio Alger.

In 1878 Hill bought a bankrupt railroad that ran up the Red River into Manitoba. He made good, of course, and in 1879 he renamed his railroad "The St. Paul, Minneapolis and Manitoba." Hill had partners in Canada, and they asked his help in building a railroad from Winnipeg to Vancouver. He laid out the line for them, and then withdrew because of the uproar over his owning a competing railroad.

Along the way, the grown-up boy who wanted to become a sea captain began to hatch an idea. The idea was to stretch a new railroad across the northern plains to the Pacific, and from there to send giant ships across the ocean to trade with the Orient. It would be nothing less than the fabled Northwest Passage.

The idea was not to make money for himself, he said, pointing out that he already had more money than he would ever need. What he wanted was the great adventure, or, as it was later labeled by others, a "stupendous goal." He would make his mark, and thousands of ordinary people would be the better for it.

All of these ideas Hill kept to himself. Lessons he had learned about outsmarting the competition stood him in good stead. In 1886 he provided money for friends in Montana to organize the Montana Central Railroad, which preempted the only feasible route from Butte to Great Falls. He expected to need it later.

The competition had its own strategy, and managed to get Hill's railroad stopped from crossing Indian land in North Dakota. Early in 1887, however, Hill got permission to cross the land if he would pay for it, and the great adventure was ready for its next phase.

Material had accumulated at Minot for some time before construction began. A lot of material. According to newspaper accounts, the road from Minot to Great Falls, 545 miles, required the following: 3,700 carloads of rails, 8,018 loads of ties, 1,223 carloads of timber, 808 of piling, 458 of lumber, 947 of spikes, and 237 of bolts. Many other supplies were required for the needs of men and animals. For example, 590,000 bushels of oats were needed to feed the work stock. The work force included 9,000 men and 7,000 horses.

The grading, which proceeded far ahead of the steel laying, was some of the hardest work. Men used oxen and plows to break the prairie sod, and wheelbarrows and shovels to move the dirt. From the mouth of the Milk River to Great Falls, grading moved along at an average of seven miles a day, with 3,300 teams of horses and 8,000 men engaged in grading. Track laying, surfacing, and the installation of piling and bridge timbers occupied an average of 225 teams and 650 men.

Ties were laid 2,800 to the mile. A day's work normally required 24 carloads of rails, 52 carloads of ties, and four carloads of timber, poles and telegraph supplies. Wagons hauled materials and supplies as far as 200 miles ahead of the steel. Missouri River steamboats hastened their own extinction by delivering materials to Coal Banks Landing and Fort Benton. As much as 15 percent of the total material was delivered by steamboat.

Permanent sidings were built about every six miles, and temporary spurs were built on the natural ground surface about every 16 miles, subject to considerable variation. These spurs were used to park trainloads of materials, and were taken up when the next spur was built.

In September 1887, a reporter for the Fort Benton *River Press* visited the construction as it neared his town. The following is the present author's edited version of his account.

> Within a couple miles of the end of the steel we saw 12 men laying ties on the grade. The ties are dropped off wagons just where they are needed within easy reach of the men who put them in position. Two men stretched a rope as a guide in placing the ties in a straight line. When the ties were properly placed on the grade, the steel could be laid on them.
>
> The engine, pushing a carload of steel before it, comes as close as it can to the end of the track. The rails are then unloaded at

the side of the track. When the rails are unloaded the train backs out and trollies that carry rails to the very end of the track are brought into position on the track next to the rails. The rails are 30 feet long and weigh 600 pounds. The steel handling gang consists of 24 men who load and unload the trollies. The rails are loaded by 18 men who stand in a line, pick up a rail, and toss it on the trolley, loading 40 rails in a few moments.

Each trolley is pulled to the end of the track by two horses that walk at the edge of the grade. Each horse is ridden by a boy. At the end of the track, 10 men, 5 on each side, push rails forward over iron rollers set in the side of the trollies for the purpose. The rails fall into their proper place, and men with width gauges measure to make sure they are in exactly the right place. When the rails are properly placed, the trolley rolls forward on them and the process is repeated.

Behind the trolley, 12 strappers place angle bars and bolt the rails together, leaving room for the rails to expand in the summer heat. Behind the strappers come four spike peddlers, 32 spike drivers, and 16 nippers. The peddlers drop the spikes at the ends of the ties. Each nipper is equipped with a steel bar attached to a wooden fulcrum. This tool is used to raise ties snug against the bottom of the rails while the spikes are being driven. Where two rails join, an extra tie is placed so each rail end rests on its own independent tie. When each trolley is unloaded, it is set off the track and another is brought up.

From 20 to 50 miles back from the end of the tracks is a gang of 500 surfacers. This gang levels up and straightens the track. Ties are adjusted, and earth from the side of the grade is thrown between them and tamped. This gang moves about as fast as the track layers, averaging 5 miles per day. When these men are finished the track is ready to receive ballast and go into service.

The reporter also described the two trains that operated at the end of the track.

At the very front of the first train is the car occupied by Donald Grant, the foreman. This car is used as an office by Grant and his clerks, other officials, and the physicians who look after the health of the men. This car also contains the post office, drug store, and a small supply store. Behind this first car are two 3-story dormitory and dining cars, followed by the cook car and two more dormitory and dining cars. The upper stories of the dining and cooking cars contain rows of bunks, uppers and lowers on each level. Back of the rear dining car is a car that answers as a blacksmith and carpenter shop. Behind this car is the supply car that carries the provisions for the dining and cooking cars. The supply car is followed by eight flatcars that carry the rails, spikes, and angle bars that are used to join the rails. The engine brings up the rear.

13

As fast as the flat cars are emptied of their materials they are backed out and sent to the rear. Loaded cars are brought up so that the train is always about the same size. A second train, the timber and steel train, moves twice a day, at noon and night. It moves empty cars back to a temporary spur referred to as the "front yard." Here it picks up loaded cars and moves them up to the front. Loaded cars can be parked at the siding nearest the front until they are needed. The front yard is kept supplied with loaded cars from Minot, and usually is between 10 and 35 miles from the front.

The movement of all the trains is regulated by telegraph. As the track moves forward, two telegraph lines move with it. One wire is for commercial use and the other strictly for railroad use. Each night the telegraph officer improvises an office at the end of the tracks, using a large box as a table for his telegraph key.

Track layers began at Minot on April 2, 1887, and entered Montana on June 13. By August, the track layers were moving at their fastest. They laid 116 miles, 3,140 feet of track that month. On August 8 near the present location of Saco they had their best day: 8 miles and 60 feet. On September 6 they were at Havre, to Fort Benton on September 28, and to Great Falls on October 15.

During construction, Jim Hill enjoyed every inch of his great adventure, riding his democrat wagon up and down along the route with his belongings in a little valise. He fraternized freely with the workers, always asking them if they were satisfied.

Generally, the workers were satisfied. They were getting $25 a month, good wages in those days. They worked six days a week, taking Sunday off to wash clothes and rest. Menial work, such as cleaning up, was performed by Chinese. One source of discontent was the clouds of mosquitoes that ate the men alive. Smudge fires were burned at night to keep mosquitos away from the sleeping cars.

The winter of 1887-1888 was not kind to the new railroad. Alternating hard freezes and chinooks caused the Milk River to flood, washing out segments of track. One three-mile section was taken out near Malta, and part of the track was found in the trees along the river 20 miles north of town.

At the time Hill built the first segment of his railroad, he did not know about the existence of the Marias Pass, though it had long been known to Indians and non-Indian travelers and residents. Unless a northern pass could be found, he would have to push southwestward from Great Falls, crossing the Rocky Mountains in the vicinity of Rogers Pass. Hill was saved from this fate by John F. Stevens, whom he had sent to find the north pass. It wasn't easy, but on December 11, 1889, under average winter conditions—four feet of snow, 40 below zero—Stevens found the pass. The special qualities of this place were later commemorated by the placement of an obelisk in the middle of the highway.

With the pass found, the great adventure could resume. Laying of the westbound track began near the site of Havre in mid-October 1890. By mid-January 1891, the track had arrived at Cut Bank, where 300 men were put to work building a trestle. The trestle was half built once, and then burned. The uncouth ancestor of modern Cut Bank grew up at the bottom of the gorge near the trestle, but flooded out that winter, and was rebuilt at its present site. The track-laying in this vicinity was said to be accompanied by saloons, gambling houses, and places of variable repute. By April 2, the trestle was completed and the track began moving west from Cut Bank.

From Cut Bank to the mountains, track moved quickly. Grading and rock cutting had been proceeding all along the route through the mountains. In the mountains, the work was hazardous, with a lot of blasting, and Chinese workers sometimes were killed or injured because they didn't speak English and didn't understand warnings. The track made it across the Rockies in 1891, to Spokane in 1892, and on January 5, 1893, the golden spike was driven in the Cascade range of Washington.

Next stop: the Orient. Jim Hill built ships for his conquest of the Orient, but his achievements there seem not to have been overwhelming. In honor of the connection, however, the train now called the *Empire Builder* was once called the *Oriental Limited.*

Back in Montana, the new railroad had effects that are well-known to most grown-up Montanans. The men building the railroad across the Hi-Line said the whole country looked like a wheat field that year, with bluejoint grass knee-high. The evident quality of the soil was part of what gave Hill confidence in Montana. Confidence in Montana!!

Without confidence in Montana, one of Hill's spokesmen said later, there would have been no Great Northern Railway. Hill's vision of the future of Montana was said to include "checker-boards of waving grain and verdant pasture, broad expanses of range, grazing cattle, abundant water for irrigation and power, lumber mills, mines for coal and other more valuable minerals, factories, thriving cities, and prosperous citizenship." All it needed was transportation.

As Hill saw it, and continually told his stockholders, the availability of efficient transportation in Montana would increase the prospects for farmers, which would bring more farming, more products shipped on the railroad, leading to greater railroad profits, which would allow the railroad to increase its efficiency, which could allow rail rates to drop, increasing farm profits, bringing in more farmers, which would bring more business to the railroad, and so on.

A hundred years later, it appears that there were some jokers in the deck. Be that as it may, the Great Northern Railway changed northern Montana forever, and will continue to have its effects. Whatever the railroad is these days, it has left behind some sentimental relics. When the Amtrak passenger is allowed off the train for 10 minutes at Havre and heads for the hot dog wagon, the shadow of a giant steam locomotive, No. 2504, looms alongside. This machine looks like a leftover from the dinosaur age, and causes young people to thank God they weren't alive to see that thing operate. Older people wish it still were operating.

And yet there's more. The Phillips County Museum in Mtten along all right with his neighbors, even if he was not a model citizen. Some-accounts say the Kid even got along okay with a local character name Pike Landusky; othes among Indian artifacts, statues from ancient Egypt, and rusty old six-shooters, one might reflect on the sweep of history and wonder what would have become of the north country if Jim Hill had not selected it for his great adventure.

HIGHWAY 2

MIGRATION ROUTE OF THE NORWEGIANS

A Norwegian friend of mine who grew up beside Highway 2 in northern Minnesota insists that the road is a legendary migration route of Norwegians. He claims that the route was pioneered by Vikings who sailed into the Great Lakes, and from there took off overland to Puget Sound.

Some versions insist they rolled their boats along, other suggest they merely walked. All Norwegians know about this migration route, my friend says. After the Vikings, Norwegians from the Old Country distributed themselves all along the road, where they remain today.

From the North Dakota line to Havre, Highway 2 follows the general route followed by Isaac Stevens in 1853, when he was looking for a wagon route for a road from St. Paul to Fort Benton. Stevens turned south just west of where Havre is and followed the approximate route of Highway 87 to Fort Benton and on to the Helena vicinity.

This route was followed by overland migrants headed for the Montana gold fields from St. Paul. In 1862 and 1863, Captain James L. Fisk led successful wagon trains over this route before Indian trouble shut down the traffic. The trail was so poorly marked that one wagon dragged a plow to make it easier for later travelers to find the route. Fisk brought a third wagon train through in 1866, and by this time the trail was much more distinct.

From its arrival in 1887 until the early 20th century, the Great Northern Railway took care of most of the Hi-Line's transportation needs. Wagon roads of the time tended to fluctuate in their passability, and were not built for speed at any rate. By the time World War I arrived, automobiles were becoming more numerous and there was a demand for passable roads. By 1913, when the legislature required cars to be registered in Montana, there were 6,000 motor vehicles in the state.

At first, the building and maintenance of public roads in Montana was the responsibility of the county commissioners, who could build whatever roads their counties could afford. The commissioners hired farmers to do the work. The state Highway Commission was created in 1913. In 1916, Congress passed a law that allowed the states to obtain federal matching funds for road construction. In 1919, efforts began to obtain funding for a highway to cross the northern part of the state from North Dakota to Idaho, a distance of about 750 miles. This was known at different times as the Glacier Park Trail, and the Teddy Roosevelt Trail. It is not clear when it became known as Highway 2.

Road building at the outset of the automotive age presented new challenges. Up to that time, macadam roads were considered state of the art. Macadam roads were built by applying crushed gravel to the roadbed, then rolling it down with heavy equipment. Fine materials were applied and compressed into the gravel. Water sometimes was used to "set the roadbed."

Macadam roads were no good for cars. Despite a series of speed limit laws that started in 1905, automobilists always liked to go as fast as they could. This speed blew all the fine materials out of the roadbed and allowed water to penetrate to the subgrade, leading to the destruction of the road. Much testing was done to determine how to build roads that could stand up to motor vehicles. Eventually the bituminous surface was developed, an early version of the asphalt roads familiar to automobilists in the second half of the 20th century.

The work on the 90 miles of the road from the Dakota line to Wolf Point probably was typical in many ways of how Highway 2 was built across the prairie portion of the state. Five contractors were to build this portion of the road, with the help of 52 subcontractors. Wages were the same as for county road work: $7 a day for a man and two horses, $10 for a man and four horses, $4 for a man with no horses. The primary work implement was the 4-horse fresno, which could move two yards of dirt. The men had to provide their own board, room, and horse feed.

The work started on that eastern stretch in the spring of 1923 and finished about a year later. The initial surface was "improved dirt." Later, gravel was added to the surface, and asphalt was applied beginning in 1934, with completion in 1936.

Travelers were always grateful for road improvements, and they also helped by developing their own sort of caution signs. A log standing up in the middle of the road, for example, indicated a hazard worthy of attention.

Early on, the Teddy Roosevelt Trail was advertised to encourage tourists. The first edition of the *Theodore Roosevelt International Highway Guide* provided a log of road conditions as they were in the summer of 1921. The log shows that conditions started good in the east. From mile 0 to mile 14 (or 732 to 746 eastbound) the first six miles were "graded and graveled, generally good," and then "improved dirt, generally good."

Between Brockton and Poplar, mile 50 to mile 64 (682 to 696), the road was "partly improved dirt, gumbo. Bad in wet weather." Gumbo and "bad when wet" cropped up intermittently as far as Bowdoin (near Malta), but west of there nearly all the road was "good," or "generally good."

H.B. Tyson, representing the Montana portion of the highway, warned in the *Highway Guide* that "The tourist must not start across Montana expecting normal road conditions. Due allowance must be made for developing conditions as they are found today."

Traveling in 1992, the tourist may expect normal road conditions on Highway 2 except during the summer, when the Highway Department will give the traveler a chance to observe the scenery while the road is blocked by construction. But that cannot be helped.

People who don't believe in progress should travel Highway 2 today. Not only is there no gumbo in the road, but the mile markers indicate that the persistent rerouting and curve straightening has knocked 79 miles off the original length of the road in Montana.

ORIGINAL OWNERS

Mark Twain once noted that in all the world, there is hardly a piece of land that is in the hands of its rightful owners. Old maps show that for a time in the late 19th century, the U.S. government acknowledged that Indians owned all the land that we refer to as the Hi-Line, from the North Dakota border of today to the Continental Divide, and from the Canadian line to the Missouri. Of course they also owned it from the time the ice went off it until the U.S. government decided the Indians didn't own it.

In the last 100 and some years, white society has been diligent in removing the vast majority of those Hi-Line acres from Indian ownership. Many white people today are seriously aggrieved that Indians were left with any land, and would relieve them from the onerous duties of ownership if they could. For the Indians' own good, of course.

The land grab was only a part of the Manifest Destiny that was foisted upon the Indians. Most elements of their culture were destroyed, and those that they managed to hold on to had to survive concerted opposition by white folks who wanted Indians to be white folks too.

In short, whites didn't do Indians any favors. Still, the Indians survived, and today show signs of cultural revival. They claim they may show white folks a few things if they get to where they deserve it. The old ways are getting more popular, the old languages are coming back, and more and more Indians are finding ways to stay Indian in a white society. One hopeful sign is the two-year community colleges that now exist on all Montana's reservations. Curricula include everything from instruction in the native culture and language to computer science. Perhaps of equal importance, these schools help ease the transition from reservation life to academic life, and many students go on to mainstream four-year colleges. Nursing, counseling, and other skills needed on the reservation are popular courses of study.

The most visible aspect of Indian cultural life on the Hi-Line is the powwow. Curly Bear Wagner, Blackfeet Cultural Coordinator, told me that among the Blackfeet, the powwow came into being to replace the Sun Dance and the Medicine Lodge Dance that white folks outlawed. At powwows, Wagner said, "We get back to the old ways for a while. We live in tipies or a tent, cook outside. People play games, dance, and get together."

The dancing is competitive, with prizes up to $2,000 awarded to the best dancer in each of six classes. "The money makes people pay attention," Wagner said. "This helps keep our culture alive."

Drummers at powwows also get paid, often $250 per drum. As a concession to the 20th century, the drums are electronically amplified. This makes powwows loud. When I asked an Indian lady for directions to a powwow, she told me just to keep my ears open. "You'll hear it before you see it," she said.

Powwows are shockingly non-commercial. You can buy jewelry or other Indian-related items at booths that get set up around the perimeter, but these merchants are mostly outsiders, and strictly soft sell. Food and soft drinks are available from vendor wagons, or sometimes for free from the hosts of the powwow. "We always treat visitors as our guests," Wagner said. "This goes back to the old days, when you visited your relatives and they would take care of you."

Along the Hi-Line, the drums sound on one or another of the reservations just about every weekend during the summer. You'll hear them before you see them. For people who are interested, powwows offer a fine introduction to the way it used to be.

OLIVER ARCHDALE

I came too early in the morning to visit Oliver Archdale at his home in Wolf Point. I had called ahead, but he hadn't taken me seriously. Archdale is a traditional Assiniboine of the Red Bottom clan, and I wanted to ask him about the significance of being an Indian.

"Indians are the opposite of white people," he said. "Indians look out for one another, treat other tribes as guests. If a white man is honored, he is given money or awards. If an Indian is honored, he has to give gifts to others, because he did not achieve his honor by himself. Indians share what they have with others, and humble themselves through prayers. For example, when an Indian takes a plate of food, he raises it a few inches off the table, as an offering."

Archdale recalled that someone high in a Presidential administration once got into a lot of trouble for saying that Indians live like Communists, but Archdale understood what he was trying to express, and said it was true. "Indians share," he said, adding, "These are cultural things that live in your heart."

Archdale said his mother was subjected to efforts to kill the Indian culture, and as a result she still refuses to disclose cultural information to any non-Indian. "We almost lost our language," Archdale said.

"They wouldn't let us speak our language in school. Now, they teach it in school."

As a youth, Archdale was not impressed with the superiority of white culture and religion. For example, he said, the school superintendent's boys were the ones who got the drunkest on Saturday night, and then in church the next day they would be hung over and faint in the heat.

Archdale filled me in on some aspects of powwows. Besides the social interaction, he said, there is the money. At the Red Bottom Celebration at Fraser, for example, the winner of each dance category receives $1,500, second place $1,000, third place $800, and fourth place $500. On one hand, Archdale said, people can use the money. On the other hand, the money detracts somewhat from the cultural basis of the dancing.

He said the Red Bottom Celebration got its start in 1903 after a man promised he would throw a celebration if his son recovered from a serious illness. The son recovered, and the first Red Bottom celebration is still talked about today.

"This man was rich," Archdale said. "He gave away wagons and teams of horses and bunches of cattle to people who needed them. So many Indians came—lots of Assiniboine from Canada—that he had to butcher four cows every day to feed them. He brought in a hay rack with 42 upright poles on it, and every pole had an eagle feather war bonnet. Today an eagle feather war bonnet is worth up to $5,000. He gave them all away. The celebration is still held every year, out of respect."

It's true, Archdale said, that some people still discriminate against Indians. "My father told me, 'Some people will be prejudiced against you, but mostly you will be treated as you deserve.' I have never forgotten that. Prejudice is a form of ignorance. I try to be courteous even to ignorant people."

Today, Archdale said, the Assiniboine are increasingly coming into their own. "People are turning back to our culture," he said. "People are becoming aware of who they are, becoming aware of how to take care of themselves. People are realizing that if they never do anything but reach for a handout, they will never go anywhere."

For his part, Archdale goes lots of places. He works as a professional pool player and organizer of pool tournaments. "I go all over the state," he said. Besides providing a livelihood, pool gives Archdale an outlet for his competitive tendencies. "It keeps me from being competitive in other things," he said.

Archdale said he might take a job that would require him to move to St. Louis. I asked him if he wouldn't feel out of place in St. Louis. "People ask me that," he said, "and I tell them, 'St. Louis is full of black people, and they come from Africa.'"

STATE LINE CASINO

Entering or leaving Montana on Highway 2 at the North Dakota line, the first or last establishment a traveler sees is the State Line Casino, about 200 yards inside Montana, just east of mile marker 667. A big sign in front of the casino has two messages. For those coming into Montana, it says "First Chance." For those leaving the state, it says "Last Chance."

Casino owner Sharon Turbiville said the "chance" offered at the casino is to play keno machines, poker, or bingo. North Dakota does not allow keno machines or poker, and its bars are shut down on Sunday. If residents of Williston, a few miles east, develop a thirst or have a vision of lucky numbers on the Sabbath, they can make a quick trip to the State Line Casino. Gambling and drinking are popular activities at the casino, Turbiville said, but the main attraction is the bargain-priced dinners. A full dinner with 12-ounce prime rib, salad, potato, and hot loaf of bread is $6.50, for example. A quarter-pound hamburger is $1.75, or $2.50 if it comes with fries. On Friday, as another example, the daily special is a 12-ounce T-bone for $3.50. Besides an assortment of sandwiches, steaks, and steak and seafood combinations, the menu offers nine different seafood entrees. "Food is how we get 'em in here," Turbiville said.

It has not always been food that brought people to the casino. "Oh, back in the fifties and sixties, they had big-time gambling here. It was one of the famous joints. They had slot machines, poker, craps, blackjack." Back in those outlaw days, Turbiville said, the casino owners had the psychic abilities that were so common among people in that business, and although the cops occasionally came to raid the place, they never found any evidence.

Across the road from the casino is an old rodeo ground grown up with weeds. Apparently there are some other facilities there too, not much used. "I put on four-wheel-drive races over there until it cost me my left arm," Turbiville said. She calculated for a moment. "And my left leg." More calculation. "About $36,000 in all." (From all appearances she still has all original arms and legs, but the $36,000 no doubt went painfully.)

Turbiville said the casino was built in the 1930s, and then burned down in the 1950s. It subsequently was rebuilt and passed through two more owners before Turbiville bought it in 1982.

On the day I was there, Turbiville was busy dragging a hose up from out back, wrestling cardboard boxes and other such stuff out of the boiler room, and hosing down the floor. I asked if I could take her picture for this book. "No," she said.

AMTRAK

Thirty years into the passenger jet age, I decided I wanted to go on a train ride. I knew just where I wanted to go: Culbertson. When I dialed 1-800-USA-RAIL, the man told me I could not go to Culbertson. "How come," I said.

"We don't go to Culbertson," he said.

"You do too," I said. "I was up there taking a picture of the depot last week and your train went through and just about blew the engineer hat right off my head."

"We go *through* Culbertson. We do not *stop* in Culbertson. As far as we are concerned here at Amtrak, there is no Culbertson."

"Well, if I can't go Culbertson, where can I go?" Choosing to pass up that opening, he said, "You could go to Williston."

"Nope," I said, "Williston is in North Dakota. As far as we are concerned here at *Montana Magazine,* there is no North Dakota." So I wound up going to Wolf Point, which is the farthest east Amtrak stops in Montana. Everybody I talked to about this trip said I should be sure to get on in Whitefish, in order to have the experience of being born again as the train bursts out of the mountains onto the plains. So I got a ticket and headed to Whitefish.

The train was supposed to leave Whitefish at 6:45 A.M., and I was there, but the train was not. My advisors had told me I could wait in the depot. They were wrong. When I got to Whitefish the night before my departure, the depot was locked up. I needed a bathroom bad. Looking around, I spotted a construction site 200 yards away with a portable toilet in its midst. This was the same sort of facility they have at rodeos, car races, and other wing-dings where you don't mind them too much because you are having so much fun. At 10 P.M. in a cold drizzle behind the depot at Whitefish, Montana, you do not have much fun. Nevertheless, the demands of the body are such that any marginally serviceable facility eventually looks like a gift from God. I slept that night in the back of my pickup, thinking for sure the depot would be open in the morning.

Wrong again. All sorts of people showed up to catch the train, and they had two questions: Why is the depot not open, and if I can't go to the bathroom in there, where can I go?

I sat on a warped bench next to the depot door to await the train. One of the many people who tried to get into the depot sat down next to me. She was about to freeze, mainly because it was cool and she was a scrawny 45-year-old wearing the clothing of a 16-year-old. Sixteen-year-olds can go nearly naked in any weather and it doesn't bother them. Forty-five-year-olds can get hypothermia looking for a beer in the refrigerator.

She seemed to suspect the closed depot was my fault. "Why is this depot not open?" she demanded.

"I don't know," I admitted.

"Is it because of the strike?" (A strike against the railroad had ended the previous day, and this was Amtrak's first run since.)

"No," I said.

"What then?"

"There is a good reason why this depot is shut down, but whatever it is is so improbable that we would never guess it in a thousand years."

"How do you know this?"

"It's got all the earmarks of one of those sorts of situations. Haven't you ever noticed that when there is something unusual and you think you know several things that might have caused it, that it is almost never one of those things?"

"No," she said. "How am I going to go to the bathroom?"

"See that construction site over there? See that little pale green house right in the middle of it?"

"I can't go over there."

"I thought you said you needed to go to the bathroom." She headed that way, shivering. Other people watched her. When she came back, these other people went over, and then some more, until all the 50 or so people waiting for the train had made the trip.

The train showed up 40 minutes late, and was almost full of irritable passengers. They were irritated even though they had been able to go to the bathroom all they wanted. The reason they were irritable was that they had been stranded during the railroad strike. One lady in my coach wanted everybody to know how annoyed she was. She'd told everybody she'd seen since she left Portland the previous day, and now she had some new people to tell. "Sure," she said with great annoyance, "they said they'd fly me.

"I told them if I wasn't petrified of flying I wouldn't be taking the train. I had to sit around Portland with nothing to do for days." And so on, and on, and on some more.

In the seat next to me was a young man from Indiana, returning from his vacation in Portland. He was mellowed out, and had no complaints. I'll call him Indiana Jones.

Jones had some observations. "One thing I like better about Montana than Oregon is that Montana doesn't have a lot of bums sleeping right beside the track. Must be too cold for 'em."

"Yep," I said. "We only have a few bums in Montana, and they are mostly all-weather bums. You won't see them sleeping beside the track."

"One thing I don't understand," Jones said. "All along the track I see this little dirt road. What is that for?"

"Actually," I said, "that only looks like a road. Actually it's a fire break."

"Ah," he said. "To keep forest fires from burning up the train."

"No," I said. "To keep the train from burning up the forest." I let him think about this for minute. He couldn't figure it out. I gave him the benefit of my vast experience. "These trains burn out their wheel bearings. Sometimes at night when you're driving along and a train goes by, you can see molten red hot metal shooting out of a burned up bearing. These hot pieces land in the dry grass and start fires. There are probably 3,000 volunteer firemen in America who would never have anything to do if it wasn't for the train starting fires." I could see Jones going away into himself because he thought he was in the company of a damned liar.

Despite this, our conversation was above average. I considered it much above that of the lady with the tirade about being stranded in Portland, for example. Eavesdropping, I noticed that most of the newly acquainted seatmates had conversations that went like this: "Hi, I'm Elsie Smith from Everett, Washington. Born and raised in Chicago, married my husband George and moved to Everett 30 years ago this month. Had six kids. They're all doing fine. George has been dead for three years. I'm on my way to Chicago to visit my oldest boy, Joe. He's in retail. Has three kids. I love all my grandkids, got 15 of 'em." And then a similar report from the other person, and then after a total acquaintance time of about 10 minutes, no more talking. Americans have short biographies.

Two young guys who got on at West Glacier had been stranded in Glacier Park during the strike, ran out of money, and spent the last couple of days huddled under a pine tree eating canned beans with a Boy Scout knife. They got some mileage out of this story. People in the adjoining seats would accost people passing through the car and say, "Ask these guys what they did in Glacier Park during the railroad strike," but after while they got tired of telling the story, gathered up their soggy baggage and went to seek anonymity elsewhere on the train.

When my seatmate and I ran out of conversation, we lapsed into silence like everybody else and I was free to evaluate the Amtrak experience. I have traveled on just about everything from mountain-grown jackass to 727, but this was my first sojourn on a modern passenger train. I noticed immediately that the ride was almost unbelievably comfortable. It was certainly the most comfortable ride I ever had. Thinking about it, I realized that no ordinary automobile is very comfortable, and airplanes certainly are not. On an airplane you are aware that you are in the grip of large horsepower, and that some of that horsepower is individually assigned to you. This power will squish you down in your seat, or push you to the left or right, make your stomach shake hands with your backbone. You may begin looking out the window and wonder how Wilbur and Orville got the ridiculous idea that a little vacuum over a wing could hold up tons and tons of heavy stuff, including yourself. No such worries on the train, which glides silently along with a feeling exactly like it should feel to ride a cloud. It pleased me to think, first, that American engineers were smart enough to make something so comfortable, and second, that responsible persons actually cared enough to make such comfort available to us, undeserving and unappreciative as we are. There's plenty of seat room, and if the person ahead of you tips the seat back, you still have plenty of space.

Presently, we exploded out onto the plains. "See that little town over there," said a slightly bewildered voice on the public address system. "That's Browning, Montana, home of the Blackfoot Nation." There was a hint of a question in the voice. Somewhere in the train, a man was speaking into a microphone, reading a script that somebody had written for him. He was wondering, "What in the hell is the Blackfoot Nation, and why am I talking about it here?"

"Sometimes in the winter we stop there, but not today," he said, still bewildered.

So we pushed on to Cut Bank. As we approached Cut Bank, a woman came on the P.A. and told us how Cut Bank got its name, and that it was an oil town. And then as we approached Shelby, the same woman treated us to a slightly fractured rendition of the Dempsey-Gibbons fight. According to her, Dempsey's manager ran off with all the money, and no purse was awarded. I fell to wondering if Amtrak would like to hire me to write their scripts.

By the time we got to Havre, the P.A. system had given up on the local color. We were just told that we were approaching Havre and if we were going to get off there we should pick up all our trash and belongings and take it with us. Also, we were allowed to get off and back on in Havre, during a 10-minute stop. This is the only place in Montana where you are allowed to get off and back on again.

Indiana Jones thought Havre was trying to fake something. He saw a big motel along the tracks and said, "I suppose they think that motel is going to fill up."

"Actually," I said, "I stay in that motel, and I can tell you that it is filled a lot of the time. It and several others in town."

He remembered his earlier impression that I was a liar. "Who by?" he asked skeptically.

"Canadians, migrating Norwegians, tourists, traveling salesmen, drug smugglers, basketball players, all sorts of folks." I could tell he didn't believe it.

Having mobbed the men's room and depleted the candy machines in the Havre depot, we reboarded and rolled on east. The P.A. announced that the bar car was open, and happy hour was upon us. The happy hour special was a strawberry daiquiri for only $2. For $2.50 you could get a beer. "Aren't you going to happy hour?" my seatmate asked. I told him that $2.50 beer did not make me happy.

We were still 40 minutes late. Some people asked the conductor if we couldn't make up some of that time. "We could," he said, "but I don't know if we will." Up front was an engineer who did what he wanted, evidently. The official schedule said we were supposed to be in Wolf Point at 3:20. Indiana took note of our continuing tardiness, and decided to cheer me up. "By four o'clock, you'll be right where you want to be," he said beaming happily at me. He seemed to think that Wolf Point was a good place for liar like me.

As we approached Wolf Point, the conductor took down the little tags above the seats of those of us who were getting off. He put up other tags that said things like, "couples only," or "groups only." I told Indiana that he should ask the conductor to put up a sign over his seat saying, "Good looking single women only." He thought that was one hell of a good idea, and began carrying on about it. "Yes, yes, eligible single women only, that's a good idea, yes, yes." He went a little overboard with it, and nearby passengers began looking at us. Directly across the aisle, a young woman traveling alone was looking at me the way she would look at vomit. We got to Wolf Point none too soon and I detrained and staggered off to a motel to make up some of the sleep I didn't get the night before.

The next day, I was back at the Wolf Point depot to await the westbound train. I thought I would be the only person boarding, but I wasn't. I had forgotten that eastern Montana consists of major geography with no transportation. To the south along the Yellowstone, there is bus service, but north of the Missouri the train is it, except for the commuter airline service that costs a lot and tends to scare people who are not crazy about flying in small craft. So people from the edges of infinity came into the Wolf Point depot and wanted to know where the train was. It was delayed somewhere down the track with a faulty switch. Everybody cleared out, some to the store to get traveling supplies, some to sit with their sweethearts out in their pickups, others to God knows where. It was just me and the station agent. "Quite the zoo you run here," I said.

"It's always like this in the summer," he said. The train turned up about 40 minutes later, and we all got on. It was much less crowded than the day before, and the "afraid to fly, bitterly disappointed in the train" group had gone off down the track. It promised to be a relaxed trip.

Somewhere west of Glasgow, the lady with the script came on the P.A. again. "South of here, between Malta and Glasgow," she said, "is what we officially call Charlie Russell Country. That's where the famous western artist spent his early days as a bronco buster and sheepherder. If you were to travel down through that area, you would see many monuments to the accomplishments of Charlie Russell, illustrator of the old west."

I reflected on the poverty of my knowledge. I have travelled through that area many times, and the only monument to Old Charlie that I am aware of is in Saco. Even that one doesn't talk about Charlie's little-known period as a sheepherder.

Presently we were back at Havre, and once again got to stop and go into the station. I was boycotting the restrooms on the train because I was under the impression that they dumped the stuff on the tracks.

When we got back to Shelby, we got an even more fractured version of the famous Dempsey-Gibbons fight. Or was it the Gempsey-Dib-

"We crush both safflower and sunflower," Kjos said. The sunflower comes from North Dakota and Minnesota. The safflower comes from Montana, North Dakota, and Canada. Most of the oil goes out in bulk, either tanker truck or rail car. "The oil can be sold either in crude form or fully refined. We can refine it right up to where it is ready for bottling," Kjos said. About half the oil is sold in crude form overseas, mostly to Japan. The remainder goes just about everyplace else in the U.S. Anybody can buy oil from SVO, bottle it under their own brand, and sell it.

"We crush between 250 and 300 tons of seed per day, seven days a week, 365 days a year. About 37 percent of the seed weight is oil. The rest is high protein feed meal that gets shipped out for cattle feed." SVO produces enough protein meal in a year at Culbertson to feed 25 million cows for a day. Or one cow for 25 million days.

Kjos said that besides crushing its own seed, the plant also contracts to extract vegetable oil from many other sources. "We've had walnuts from California, peach pits, sesame seed, avocado...we can crush about anything."

Zane Panasuk, merchandiser at the Culbertson plant, is upbeat about the future of the plant, and about Montana safflower oil. "The safflower oil produced in Montana is the best in the world. It is the lowest in saturated fats, for example."

Panasuk said the production of oil in Culbertson has a lot of potential for business in Montana. "Somebody should start bottling safflower oil and sunflower oil in Montana," he said. He cited canola oil as another business opportunity. Much of the canola oil purchased in Montana, and elsewhere, is produced at Culbertson, then shipped to Idaho where it is bottled and sold. "If they can do it in Idaho, we should be able to do it in Montana."

Panasuk said that safflower has fit itself into Montana agriculture in the last 40 years. Farmers need a crop that can grow as a complement to their grain rotation, and break up the disease and insect cycles that result from growing wheat on the same ground year after year. "Grain farmers have always needed a second crop. They tried mustard, sunflower, and canola, without much success. They needed a crop that was as easy to grow as wheat. Safflower is the answer. It needs a little more management. Seed placement is more critical, and it won't grow if it is planted too deep, or if the soil crusts over." These are not serious problems. "We have one grower who has contracted with us for the past 25 years. His dollars returned have been greater than they would have been for wheat." Panasuk said that growing safflower costs about $10 or $12 more per acre than growing wheat. On the other hand, safflower produces about the same seed volume as wheat, and the price is usually higher. In the spring of 1992, the price was $4.40 a bushel, while wheat hovered around $3.00.

"There's definitely a market for safflower oil. The big oils keep going down and down and down, and safflower keeps going up," Panasuk said.

Safflower also fits into the time schedule of a wheat farm, in that it is harvested later than wheat. Most growers plant safflower in their grain stubble from the previous year, rather than summer fallowing it. This has benefits, Panasuk said. "Say you have a piece of ground with grassy weeds. Safflower is a broadleaf, so you can plant it in there and use an herbicide that will take out the grassy stuff."

Safflower is a good plant to grow in dry times. It has a long tap root, and can use moisture that is out of reach for grain. It likes arid country. "It won't stand much rain," Panasuk said.

About 150,000 acres of safflower is grown on the Northern Great Plains. A similar amount is grown in California by a Japanese company. "We'd like to contract 200,000 acres," Panasuk said. "Montana farmers have not been very supportive. We contract three times as many acres in North Dakota as in Montana. Look down here at Beach, North Dakota. [He pointed at a map.] I can go down to Beach, and in one day I can sign up 5,000 acres. Just across the line from there in Montana, I could sit there all year and not sign up 5,000 acres. The conditions are the same, everything is the same, except the farmers. Don't ask me why. Maybe it's because the farmers making the decisions in North Dakota tend to be younger and more open to new ideas. I don't know."

The best quality safflower seed comes from the Golden Triangle, Panasuk said. Besides taking seed from North Dakota and Montana, SVO contracts safflower 150 miles into Canada. "We're located here because this is a safflower growing area," Panasuk said.

He noted the significance of the mill to the local economy. "We pay $100,000 in taxes in this county. Our payroll is $50,000 a month. We employ forty people. Our natural gas bill is $10,000 a month."

He said that Montana doesn't do much to encourage business. "It probably would pay to pick this plant up and move it into North Dakota, just to get the benefits and tax breaks." That's not going to happen though, he said.

One thing's for sure, they're not just a grain elevator.

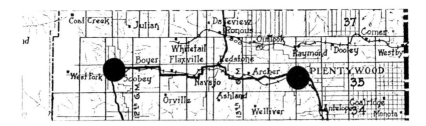

PLENTYWOOD & SCOBEY

One book about Plentywood is called *Plentywood Portrait: Soil, Toil, and Oil,* which may not make the town sound like the sort of place you'd like to read about, much less visit. Actually, Plentywood's history is a lot more complex than the title suggests. In place of soil, toil, and oil, you could refer, in approximate order, to Indians, cowboys, outlaws, homesteaders, Communists, newspaper wars, baseball wars, bootleggers, moonshiners, pimps and car thieves. All these things are past, but the oil, soil and toil remain, at least in part. Oil is not doing much these days because of low prices, and a lot of the soil is in the Conservation Reserve Program (CRP)—son of "soil bank"—which keeps it growing grass. Besides saving the soil, this reduces the toil, although implement dealers and others are not too happy about it.

The history of white people got an early start in the northeast corner of the state when the steamboats came up the Missouri on their way to Fort Benton. However, the steamboat traffic did not produce many permanent residents in the area. When the vigilantes were stretching their ropes in Bannack and Virginia City, the bunchgrass was sighing in the wind of the northeast, and the Indians were still hunting buffalo. It wasn't until the buffalo were gone and the Indians subdued in the 1880s that cattlemen came seeking grass. Permanent settlement was still farther down the road. The town of Plentywood was not incorporated until 1912, when growth was booming as a result of railroad construction and the homesteader influx.

The town of Plentywood was named after Plentywood Creek, which runs into Big Muddy Creek at the town site. Plentywood Creek got its name from Dutch Henry, a cowboy who became exasperated at watching the chuckwagon cook trying to cook dinner using wet buffalo chips for fuel. After enduring this spectacle as long as he could, Henry jumped up and said "If you'll go two miles farther up this creek, you'll find plenty wood."

Henry came to Montana with a herd of longhorns from Texas, and eventually became a famous member of a populous horse-thief fraternity in the northeast corner of Montana. He was reputed to steal horses in Montana and drive them into Canada, sell them, then steal them again and drive them back down and sell them in North Dakota. He disappeared at some point and, in the manner of all famous outlaws, was reported to have been killed twice in two different places and times (in Canada); on another occasion his body was positively identified in Minnesota; he was reported hanged for rustling in Mexico; and was said to have lived as a happily married man until 1929, when he died of a gunshot wound. No explanation was offered regarding circumstances of this shooting.

At any rate, those who squint over the nearby treeless plains and surmise that the name Plentywood is some sort of sarcasm have Henry to thank. There is no indication that Henry had anything to do with naming No Wood, Wyoming, which stands next to a forest.

The abundance of outlaws in the late 1890s and early 1900s was common to all the northeast country including the vicinity of Plentywood and Scobey. Many of these individualists evidently were cowboys who came up from Texas with the longhorns, and finding no work to their liking, hit the owlhoot trail. In the 1890s, a stock inspector said that Valley County (before Sheridan and Daniels counties were split off) "is the most lawless and crookedest county in the union, and the Big Muddy is the worst part of it." Local pride suggests he was referring to the Plentywood district. Besides Dutch Henry there were Horsethief Jones, Kid Trailer, the Pigeon-Toed Kid, The Norse Brothers, and many others who allegedly practiced theft and consumer fraud with horses on both sides of the international border. According to one report, these thieves did not usually bother the local people, and if they did steal a local horse they could sometimes be persuaded to return it. The outlaws were said to be courteous to women, and if they stopped in a homestead shack when no one was there they always left it in good order. When horse thieving got unprofitable, the outlawry died down until the 1920s, of which more later.

Scobey was named after Charles Richardson Anderson Scobey, Indian agent at Poplar from 1889 until 1907. Scobey developed from a cattle ranch on the Poplar River 14 miles south of Canada and 60 miles west of North Dakota. The ranch began in 1902. A spur line of the Great Northern Railway reached Scobey in 1913. On Thanksgiving Day that year, the first train arrived. There was only one saloon in town, but the celebration that accompanied the train provided plenty of business. One account noted that the Greek workers who had laid the rails and driven the spikes "joined the hilarity with drink and knife fights."

Scobey continued to grow, and was incorporated in 1916. In 1920 Daniels County split from Valley and Sheridan counties, and Scobey became the county seat.

As the homesteaders came in, numerous other communities sprang up in the area surrounding Plentywood and Scobey. A few of these were Dooley, Mondak, Antelope, Homestead, Medicine Lake, Froid, Dagmar, Outlook, Comertown, Peerless, and Flaxville. Among the things the newcomers needed was news. Every little town liked to have its own newspaper, and Sheridan County at its peak had 20 such sheets. These included the Plentywood *Herald,* the Medicine Lake *Wave,* the Antelope *Independent*—formerly the *Argus,* the Coalridge *Call,* the Dagmar *Record,* the Redstone *Review,* the Raymond *News,* the Dooley *Sun,* the *Sheridan County Farmer,* the Outlook *Optimist,* the Outlook *Promoter,* the Homestead *Pioneer,* the Westby *News, The Liberator* of Archer, *The Record* of Daleview, the *Sheridan County News,* and the Plentywood *Pioneer Press.* (Also included was the author's favorite newspaper name, the Homestead *Broadaxe).* Of all these fine journals, only the Plentywood *Herald* survives in 1992. Similarly, most of the communities where they were published now exist only in history.

As the seats of adjoining counties, Plentywood and Scobey developed a vigorous rivalry that reached its peak in the 1920s. This rivalry can be seen in two newspapers from the time, the *Producers News* of Plentywood, and the *Daniels County Leader* from Scobey. The goings-on of the '20s provided a perfect backdrop for the feuding between the two editors, each of whom accused the other of contributing to community sordidness. An objective opinion that probably applied to both communities was written in the 1970s by a survivor of those times. Magnus Aasheim, in *Sheridan's Daybreak,* a history of Sheridan County, wrote "The 'roaring twenties' struck Plentywood as it did every other city. The hills were full of stolen cars and whiskey hijackers. Straw piles revealed cars hidden from the law. The 'Red' faction invaded our territory. Burning crosses were seen in the countryside."

The mention of "the Red faction" refers to the Plentywood newspaper, the *Producers News,* and its Communist editor, Charley "Red Flag" Taylor. Apparently it took a combination of hard times and the political nonconformity of people in the Plentywood area to bring Taylor to Montana. The nonconformity showed up early in a mild form when the county endorsed Teddy Roosevelt's split from the Republican Party in 1912. This nonconformist tendency built up steam from 1916 to 1921, when drought and crop failure led to the organization of Socialist groups throughout the county. Beginning in 1917, the Nonpartisan League spilled over from North Dakota. The League advocated abolition of taxes on farm improvements and state ownership of elevators and flour mills.

Socialists and League supporters joined forces in 1918 to found a newspaper in Plentywood. League headquarters in Minnesota chose the editor, Charley Taylor, a Socialist from Minnesota. The *Producers News* began printing in April, and went to almost every house in the county. Partly because of the *News'* influence, the Nonpartisan League candidates were elected that year to every Sheridan County office except state senator and superintendent of schools.

The Communists had only recently taken over in Russia, and Taylor was not slow in announcing that he and the *Producers News* were in support of Communist ideology. Socialists won every county office in 1922 and 1924, and lost only that of superintendent of schools in 1926.

The Sheridan County sheriff elected in 1922 was Rodney Salisbury, a Socialist crony of Taylor's. During his tenure from 1922 to 1928, Sheridan County was a haven for members of the Industrial Workers of the World, known as IWW or "Wobblies." The county also had a reputation of being wide open to gambling, bootlegging, prostitution, and other profitable vices. Plentywood had at least six illegal joints, and every outlying town had at least one. The village of Outlook even had a roulette wheel. Occasionally there were arrests for such activities, but the assumption was that those arrested had failed to pay the sheriff adequately.

Taylor had difficulty seeing illegal activities in Sheridan County, but he could see them plainly in Daniels County. In one article regarding a raid by federal agents in Scobey, the large headline in the *Producers News* read, "Booze Flows in the Streets of Scobey—Wild Orgy of Outlawry in Border Town—Temporarily Stopped by Federal Agents."

The editor of the Daniels County paper had a different view, noting that six saloons had been raided in Plentywood, compared to only one in Scobey. His headline said, "Producers News' Pet Bootleggers Jailed."

Taylor and his stooge Salisbury also liked to needle the editor of the *Daniels County Leader,* Burley Bowler, and the sheriff of that county. In one typical article, Taylor referred to Bowler as a "common ordinary draft dodger, deadbeat and saloon bum." Under the headline, "Scobey Sheriff Pulls Another Fool Stunt," Taylor explained that he used that headline so frequently that he was just going to keep it set in type for the many future occasions when he was sure to need it.

Back in Scobey, Bowler derided Taylor and his cohorts as "the Sheridan Soviet and Hijackers Union." He suggested their occupations were suspect. "No one ever caught one of them doing real work, but they live good, drive fine cars, and are always as sleek and fat and well-dressed as tin horns who pay them money for protection."

In one of his many articles about cars being stolen in Scobey, Taylor wrote that the latest theft "was about the 94th car" stolen in Scobey. He went on to write that "Insurance company adjusters state that more cars disappear in Scobey every year than in any other center of like population in the United States, and few are recovered."

Bowler, on the other hand, wrote that Plentywood "maintains its record as home of practically all cars stolen in the west, more than a score being located in Plentywood in the past few months."

In one of his more clearly entertaining moods, Taylor had fun with a Plentywood lawyer who advertised himself as a *Norsk Advocat,* Norwegian lawyer, appealing to the Norwegian population for business. Taylor referred to him as a *Norsk abekat,* Norwegian monkey, which gave high entertainment to the Norwegians. Clearly, one did not have to be a Communist to enjoy reading the *Producers News.*

Although he was an outspoken advocate of the rights of international workers and other big causes, editor Taylor sometimes took a wrathful approach to small offenses, such as failing to advertise in his newspaper. In one famous event, a local restaurant stopped advertising in the *Producers News*, and a front page news story soon appeared stating that cockroaches had been found in the restaurant's food. To top this off, one of Taylor's stooges waited for a busy time in the restaurant and then showed off a mouse which he said he had just found in his soup. References to this mouse appeared in the *Producers News* for the next two years.

In his role as a senator in the state legislature, Taylor often was at odds with the Anaconda Copper Mining Company and its supporters, who were said to "wear the copper collar." For a time, the Anaconda Copper Mining Company advertised in the *Producers News,* and was safe from attack by the paper, but then it dropped its advertising. In the first issue after the disappearance of the Anaconda ads, Taylor announced a powerful aversion to "The Company," referring to it as "the enemy of popular government."

Taylor frequently used his news and editorial columns for personal attacks against people who had annoyed him. One account said he "launched campaigns of out-and-out criminal libel against dozens of persons." One of his staff who abandoned him to join a rival paper was said to have been seen crawling out a woman's bedroom window; a local surgeon was accused of kidnapping a patient; a resident of a nearby community who had lent money to the *Producers News* organization and wanted it back was accused of having moral responsibility for the recent deaths of two members of his family, and the *News* suggested he should be at least mobbed, if not lynched.

The *Daniels County Leader* was not the only rival paper that felt Taylor's displeasure. He referred to a rival Plentywood paper as "that nauseous rag that emits itself once a week from its sty down the street." He may have been referring to the Plentywood *Herald,* which routinely opposed the positions taken by the *Producers News.* Making himself perfectly clear, Taylor wrote that the editor of the *Herald* was "a moral leper, a corrupt degenerate, a faker, liar, and fraud."

The *Producers News* thrived during the twenties despite the good times that resulted from good farm crops and good prices. Political theorists suggest that many farmers had been permanently damaged by the poor crops and low prices in the late teens and early '20s, and this is why they remained loyal to the *News* and its radical philosophy. There are other possible reasons for the paper's popularity. For one, the whole country was on a sort of party during the Roaring Twenties, Montana included, and the *Producers News* was fun to read, a sort of party sheet itself. Contrasted to most of the little papers put out in the surrounding communities, it was a professional product; besides the Communist editorials, it was full of local news, and was laid out like a big city daily paper. As long as the party lasted, the paper had a readership.

Grain production in the northeast counties reached almost legendary proportions in the mid-1920s. In 1924, Scobey claimed to be the largest single primary wheat loading center in the U.S., loading 2,750,000 bushels. This resulted partly from a bumper crop, partly from Scobey being the end of the railroad spur that year, and partly from the smuggling of a lot of wheat from Canada to take advantage of a better price in the U.S. The rail spur was extended to Peerless the following year, and to Opheim in 1926. By 1992, the segment of this spur between Scobey and Opheim was being considered for dismantling.

In 1925, the *Producers News, Daniels County Leader,* and all the other newspapers in the vicinity had major sporting news. Scobey, "the ancient enemy of Plentywood in the baseball world," as the *News* said, made up its mind to field a team that would overwhelm the competition. According to some accounts, Plentywood started this baseball war by hiring a black man named John Donaldson, an over-aged pitcher from the semi-pro leagues. Donaldson was said to be a very tall man, with long arms that reached below his knees. John McGraw of the New York Giants reportedly said that Donaldson would have been worth a million dollars if he could have been whitewashed. That was earlier in his career. By 1925, Donaldson was no longer a kid. Some said he was over 40 years old, but he was still big stuff in Plentywood. Burley Bowler wrote that Plentywood might have a chance if the Ku Klux Klan didn't chase their pitcher back to Alabama. Seeking to liven up the sports copy, Bowler in one headline referred to Donaldson as "The Flinging Son of Ham," referring to the old idea that black people were descended from Ham, the son of Cain. There was an active chapter of the KKK in the vicinity, and though they occasionally burned crosses and threatened to take over the government, they never bothered the black pitcher, as far as the record shows.

To counter Plentywood's treachery in hiring a former semi-pro player, the Scobeyites began casting about for available baseball talent. They came up with two members of the Chicago White Sox who were disgraced for throwing the World Series in 1919, Swede Risberg and Happy Felsch. As long as they were at it, they rounded up a whole contingent of other semi-pro or professional players who were washed up in the big leagues or otherwise at loose ends.

Risberg was hired first, and he summoned Felsch, who was delivered to Bainville on the Oriental Limited. Supporters met Felsch at Bainville and hustled him to Plentywood where he was barely in time for his first game on his new team. He put on his Scobey uniform in the dugout. According to unbiased accounts, the presence of Risberg and Felsch and the other ringers was as much a surprise to Scobey fans as to Plentywood. Scobeyites, even without knowing about the ringers, had taken all the bets they could get on their team. When Scobey won, 4-2, it was estimated that the Scobeyites came home with about $6,500 of Plentywood money. In 1992, Larry Bowler, son of Burley and his successor as publisher of the *Daniels County Leader,* remembered the financial windfall. "You had to bet on your home team, and when they lost the whole town was half-ass devastated." Scobey won every game but three that year, even on a barnstorming tour far afield in other states and provinces.

Swede Risberg was paid $600 a month, and the *Producers News* referred to him disparagingly as "the $1,500 pitcher," and "one of the outlaws from the Chicago White Sox." Scobey businessmen put up $4,300 a month to meet team payroll and expenses. The newspapers in 1925 advertised new cars for around $500, giving an idea of what kind of money was at stake.

Risberg had been a shortstop for the White Sox, but worked as a pitcher for the Scobey Giants (later referred to in a memoir by Burley Bowler as "the off-colored Scobey Sox"). He normally pitched until the score was safely lopsided and then let someone else pitch. Some opposing teams were so hopeless that each of the Giants took a turn pitching.

Larry Bowler told me in 1992, "The hardest thing [about Felsch and Risberg] was getting them on the field sober. They liked to get drunk and scrap with the local toughs and practice their fastballs by throwing rocks at our streetlights." Not that the local toughs were seriously disadvantaged. "They gave good account of themselves," Bowler said with hometown pride.

The following year, Felsch was back as manager of the Giants, but Risberg was gone, Donaldson apparently was gone from the Plentywood team, and the magic of 1925 was no more. Given the abundant grain harvests and the triumph of the Scobey Giants, 1925 should have been a favorite year for many Scobeyites, if their cars didn't get stolen.

By the end of the twenties, the people of Sheridan County had several good harvests behind them, and apparently they were tired of personal attacks and other antics by Charles Taylor. In the 1928 elections, the Republicans took every office in the county except for those won by two independents and one Democrat. The Stock Market crash of 1929 and the return of the drought gave Taylor hope that the tough times would help him recoup his political losses. To forestall this, the Democrats and Republicans joined forces (an act that old-timers still refer to as the "unholy alliance"), and defeated the Communists at the polls. A total of 575 voters in the county chose the straight Communist ticket that year. That election also brought Franklin Roosevelt to the Presidency, and his New Deal addressed many of the problems that had made the Communists popular in Sheridan County for 20 years. The *Producers News* lasted until 1937, but never regained its old influence.

Charles Taylor and Burley Bowler both died in 1967. Taylor went first, on May 25, and left Bowler with the last word. Bowler wrote of his old adversary, in part: "An old friend, a bitter opponent, a colorful character and one of the most talked-about, abused and abusive scribes of his day passed on a few weeks ago. Of course we refer to Charley 'Red Flag' Taylor, the first and long-time editor of the *Producers News* at Plentywood. Charley was no ordinary country editor."

Bowler died on December 18 that year.

Today, Plentywood and Scobey are calm little towns on the prairie with no outward sign of their former rowdiness. In good years, the elevators still load plenty of wheat, although one of them now is owned by the Japanese. Ranching and farming are still the economic backbone, according to Joe Nistler, news editor of the Plentywood *Herald*. I asked Nistler if there was any trace of the agrarian radicalism from earlier days.

"Nope. A while back The National Farmers Organization [the nearest thing to a radical farm organization in 1992] tried to recruit here and there wasn't any interest."

Nistler said Canadian trade also is important. An article in the *Herald* said that Plentywood banks handled almost $1.8 million in Canadian funds in 1991. This was a 52 percent increase from 1990, and almost 70 percent up from 1989.

Many Canadians come down from Regina to drink and gamble on the weekends, but Nistler said most of them "make a left turn" and go to North Dakota where $2 blackjack is legal. Canadians cannot get enough blackjack. State authorities raided Plentywood for illegal gambling in the early 1980s. "It wasn't a pretty sight," he said.

Nistler said most of the people still living in and around Plentywood are hanging on by their fingernails. He cited the Conservation Reserve Program (CRP) as one of the things driving the community down. "When farmers get paid for not farming, they don't need the things they would need if they were farming. A lot of the older farmers are just taking retirement at government expense. We have a big colony of snowbirds who go south in the winter." He said that the county has its maximum allowable acreage, one quarter of the county, 168,000 acres, in CRP. This has had its effects on Main Street. "We have one implement dealer now, where we had two or three 10 years ago."

In some ways, Nistler said, the problems of Plentywood are the same as the problems of the rest of country. "We're not lazy and we're not lacking in brain power," he said, adding that the lack of opportunity makes Plentywood, along with the rest of the state, an exporter of brains and muscles. Back in the late 1970s and early 1980s, he said, the economic activity generated by the oil boom raised expectations and a lot of people who had left Plentywood came back, showing that people would like to return if they could.

Nowadays, the people around Plentywood are looking for ways to make ends meet. One going concern is the raising of exotic and game animals. A brochure from the Mon-Dak Game Breeders Association in Plentywood shows that animals raised in the area include pygmy goats, fainting goats, angora goats, fallow deer, eland (large African antelope), llamas, cashmere goats, yaks, pot-bellied pigs, miniature horses and donkeys, Nubian ibex, Bezor goats, blackbuck antelope, mouflon sheep, Barbados sheep, aoudad sheep, alpacas, rheas, nilgai, muntjac deer, ostriches, and Romanov sheep, not to mention elk, white-tailed deer, and mountain lions.

Nistler pointed out that Plentywood's ties to Canada are two-way, and more than economic. "We're two hours from Regina. Regina has a professional football team, a fantastic center of the arts, concerts, shows by major artists." Also, some Americans take advantage of Canada's medical system, he said. For example, dentures are much cheaper in Canada than in the U.S.

Some of the Canadian/American activities in Plentywood are reminders of the old sporting days of the '20s. "I wish you could see this place during our fastpitch softball tournaments," Nistler said. "The whole town is wall-to-wall cars." Plentywood has two fastpitch teams that play in a league with teams from small towns in Canada. One of the tournaments held in Plentywood has been going on for 35 years and hosts 24 teams.

The town also plays host to a hot-air balloon rally each summer, with balloons from the U.S. and Canada.

Nistler said Plentywood's isolation doesn't leave it much hope for the Great American Dream of a small clean industry to bring jobs. "We're going to have to hold onto our basics, take advantage of the Canadian exchange rate when we can, and scrape by," he said.

In Scobey, Larry Bowler echoed some of Nistler's comments. "CRP knocked hell out of small communities," he said. Despite CRP and other annoyances, Bowler was optimistic. "Some retired people are coming back here because of the low real estate prices. Canadians are coming down more and more to buy groceries and other stuff. A pack of Camels costs them $6.80 in Coronach, so they're going to keep coming. They like to bring their motor homes down and spend some time on our golf course."

Scobey doesn't have any oilfields nearby, and with no boom, there was no bust. "It was hard on Plentywood and Glasgow," Bowler said, "but it never got abnormal around here."

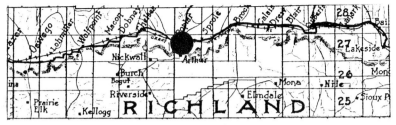

POPLAR

A & S TRIBAL INDUSTRIES

Ask anybody, "Where is the largest manufacturing plant in Montana?" Very few residents of the overpopulated districts, such as Billings, Missoula, Great Falls, and Butte, are likely to answer "Poplar." Nevertheless, since its beginning in 1974, A & S Tribal Industries, a business owned by the Assiniboine and Sioux tribes of the Fort Peck Reservation, has grown to the biggest operation of its kind in Montana. Begun with the intent of bringing employment to the reservation, this facility has expanded until in 1992 it occupies 185,000 square feet.

Up until 1992, A & S worked primarily to fill government contracts for camouflage netting and watertight aluminum medical chests. A & S has employed up to 575 people, although employees were down to about 250 after completion of camouflage netting contracts when I visited in March of 1992. Another 50 people were laid off later that year.

Dave Christianson, Engineering and Plant Program Manager for the plant, was optimistic despite the slowdown in business. At my second visit to the plant, Christianson said that the company had submitted bids on jobs totalling over $23 million, and he was confident that A & S would win some of these and that business would pick up. To improve the long-term prospects, he said, the plant managers were hoping to reduce their dependence on defense contracts and to move more into contracts with private business. One promising possibility is the manufacture of netting to keep birds and wildlife out of waste ponds generated by oil development and mines. Christianson said that it all depends on the direction taken by federal officials. He said, "If they decide to weaken the [environmental] regulations, then we won't be selling much netting for these purposes. If they get tough, it will be good for us."

Entering onto the plant floor at A & S is a humbling experience. Enormous machine presses, some of them more than two stories high, stand in a long double line. Workers, mostly Indians, move around at floor level, operating the big machines. On the larger presses, gear wheels six or eight feet across turn with enormous force, activating the presses that cold-form aluminum sheets in their various stages on the way to becoming medical chests.

Christianson said the plant has 36 machine presses ranging in capacity from 10 to 525 tons, and including single-acting presses, double-acting presses, hydraulic and computer operated units. The workers hustle on the job. "We have an incentive program," Christianson said. "The more they do, the more they get paid.

"Our first goal is to employ people. We also are profit oriented. We are a corporation wholly owned by the Assiniboine and Sioux Tribes. [In 1991] our sales were seventeen and a half million dollars. Normally they would be around twenty million." Payroll in 1991 totaled $5.5 million.

A & S trains its own employees, partly through on-the-job training. As of March 1992, trainees were paid $4.53 an hour. This trainee status lasts 90 days, after which the employees become eligible for incentive pay for production above a certain level. The pay scale rises with seniority, and production workers can eventually make up to $12 or $13 an hour. After three years on the job, workers qualify for a pension. "We have a good retirement program," Christianson said.

"Ten percent or so of the work force comes and goes," Christianson said, but most of the employees are faithful workers. "There are people who have worked here since the plant opened."

The presence of the plant also has indirect effects on the economy. "In a normal year we buy a million and a half dollars worth of materials locally," Christianson said. "Construction materials, that sort of thing. Indian-owned businesses get preference if they are within 10 percent of the low bid."

An element of uncertainty accompanies A & S's role as a supplier of military equipment. In times of military activity, things bustle. During the war with Iraq (January to March 1991) the plant ran three shifts six days a week. It normally runs three shifts a day five days a week. These three shifts usually produce 400 medical chests a day, though production reached 2,400 a week during the war with Iraq. When the war was over, things went back to normal. In 1992, the company was wondering how it would be affected by military cutbacks.

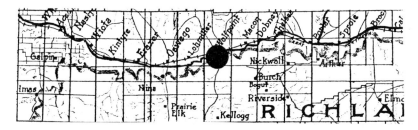

WOLF POINT

The state of New York has West Point, but Montana has Wolf Point. Elementary students in a one-room school where I matriculated always got confused over the difference between the two. I have since concluded on the whole that I would rather go to Wolf Point than West Point.

All students of Montana lore know that Wolf Point got its name from some wolves that were harvested by wolfers and apparently froze before they could be skinned. Steamboatmen saw the wolves and named the point of land "Wolf Point." The early town was a frontier village that featured a dugout hotel by the river.

With the decline of steamboating and wolfing came the big cattle herds, which had their brief hour. It was homesteading that gave the town life. By 1913, the dugout was out of business and banks and grain elevators came to town. In 1914, a land drawing was held to open the Fort Peck Reservation to homesteading by non-Indians, and the land was taken up in the following three years. After that, farming proceeded apace, up and down with weather and prices, in the familiar fashion.

In 1992, the descendants of the original banks and elevators are still fixtures in town. An ordinary eyeball measurement indicates that the elevators in Wolf Point may be the biggest along the Hi-Line. Two banks hold down street corners with a substantial cash ballast extracted from the surrounding farmlands.

Greg Little is editor of the *Herald News* in Wolf Point. I visited him to get an objective view of the Wolf Point situation. It turned out that Greg was new on the job, having only recently arrived from the Midwest. He was excited at being back in journalism after having worked in another job, and he was excited about Wolf Point. He pointed out that the town has a new twin theater, and is home to many fine artists whose work probably will become known with time.

Later that year the Fort Peck Tribal Council tentatively agreed to allow construction of a substantial gambling complex on the reservation. The location being considered is at the junction of Highway 2 and Highway 13, about 7 miles east of Wolf Point. If this project is built, it could employ as many as 500 local people, adding a whole new aspect to the economic scene.

For the time being, Little said, the town is concentrating on modest proposals for economic development. For example, the Missouri Valley Development Corporation (MVDC) and the Assiniboine Tribe worked together to set up a traditional village near the river outside Wolf Point. The idea was to charge tourists for a tour of the village. During the summer, the village consisted of 19 tipis, a sweat lodge, a buffalo surround of the sort the Assiniboine used before they had horses, an eagle trap, and various other traditional features. A member of the Assiniboine Tribe, Oliver Archdale, was in charge of the village. He said the village is as much for his own people to help preserve their old ways as for tourists.

MVDC also is considering plans for a museum next to Highway 2 outside Wolf Point. Studies show that more than 200,000 nonresidents travel Highway 2 through Wolf Point each year, and the town would like to slow them down long enough to get a little money out of them. A museum by the highway might work. As initially envisioned, the museum would comprise three parts, one Native American, one with the history of non-natives in the vicinity, and one a tractor collection. Little said a local man has "an ungodly number" of John Deere tractors that he has collected and might be willing to display at the museum.

In theory, tourists who stop to look at the museum might be interested in visiting the Assiniboine village or taking part in other activities, such as rides on a pontoon boat on the river, or a wagon train that MVDC is considering.

Such efforts should be able to generate a little more economic activity in Wolf Point, but nothing equalling the current importance of the grain elevators and banks in town.

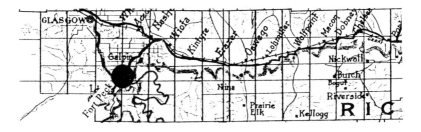

FORT PECK

One of the planetary features visible from earth orbit is Fort Peck Reservoir. If the earthbound traveler takes State Highway 117 from its intersection with Number 2 just west of Nashua, he or she will come presently into view of a horizon that seems perfectly flat. A road runs along the crest of this horizon, with street lights alongside. Tourists often drive across in search of Fort Peck Dam. Sometimes they can't find the dam, partly because they are confused when they find the dam's concrete spillway all by itself three miles away. Occasionally these would-be sight-seers suspect they have been swindled somehow and they get irate. "Where is Fort Peck Dam?" they demand. "Why, it's that flat thing you just drove across," they are told. "Don't look like no dam to me," they say.

It's true that Fort Peck is no Hoover, no Grand Coulee, but it's ours and we are proud of it. How many times does the average Montanan in his or her life hear the words, "Largest earthfill dam in the world?" Any greenhorn who has not heard these words is not a fully initiated resident.

As the world gets more overbuilt, Fort Peck loses a little of its distinction. Now it's the third largest earthfill dam, the Russians and Pakistanis having surpassed it. But, it is still the largest "hydraulically filled earthfill dam."

Let us look back to 1933. It had long been known that there was a suitable site for a dam on the Missouri two or three miles below the location of the old Indian trading post of Fort Peck, the remains of which had long since eroded into the river. The mayor of Glasgow, Leo B. Coleman, visited the proposed dam site and made himself famous by estimating it might cost a million dollars to build a dam there. In those days, a million dollars was the most money a lot of people could imagine. The Corps of Engineers had looked at the site, but didn't recommend a dam be built, and didn't want to build one there. Nevertheless, in Washington, D.C., two powerful men were thinking about such a dam. The first man was Burton K. Wheeler, U.S. Senator from Montana, whose help was needed by the second man, President Franklin Roosevelt. Roosevelt needed to do a favor for Wheeler, Wheeler needed to do something for the economy in Montana.

Meanwhile, depression and drought had hold of the country, and people were desperate to improve conditions. One improvement that was widely advocated was the construction of dams. The Agricultural Extension Service in Bozeman was putting out brochures encouraging farmers to dam their coulees and showing them how to do it. Here and there around the state, farmers who thought of themselves as radicals were meeting in country school houses and haranguing each other about the need for big dams on all the rivers, including the Missouri. These dams, they said, were the key to economic recovery and prosperity.

When all of these influences worked together, the Corps of Engineers soon found itself with a dam to build. Authorization came on October 14, 1933. Nine days later, 70 local recruits, dryland farmers who had busted, showed up to start clearing brush and cutting timber in the area to be occupied by the dam and reservoir. The Corps bought every ax, shovel, saw, and mattock in Glasgow and ordered half a railroad car more. Pay for laborers was 50 cents an hour, and hiring preference was given to men from the surrounding counties.

Not all the work could be done by local people, however. For example, in January 1934, the shipbuilders arrived to begin work on the "Fort Peck Navy." This fleet, mostly built on site, consisted of the following:

Four 40x70-foot dredges, each with five 2,500-horsepower motors

Four floating booster barges, each with two 2,500-horsepower pumps

387 pontoons for floating the 28-inch diameter pipelines from the dredges

Two hundred pontoons to hold the power cables leading to the dredges

Four swing wire pontoons

Four work barges .

Three hand barges with 40-horsepower gas winches

Two derrick boats, each with 25-ton lifting capacity

Four anchor barges

Eight landing barges for pipelines

Four pump barges to operate in the core pool

Two ferry barges

Six 100-horsepower gasoline launches with 40-foot hulls

Three 65-horsepower launches

Besides this assemblage, the *John Ordway,* a 210-horsepower diesel towboat, became probably the last sternwheel boat to make it up the Missouri, making the 2,000-mile trip from St. Louis to Fort Peck between June 1934 and May 18, 1935, laying over the winter in North Dakota.

One of the first orders of business was to clear the damsite. Bulldozers, draglines and earthmovers were brought in to level the spot. When this was complete, sheet-steel pilings were driven from the surface to a depth where they penetrated the water-impervious Bearpaw Shale below.

At about the same time that the pilings were being driven, railroad trestles were built high above what was to be the upper (upstream) and lower "toes" of the dam. These toes were to be made of gravel. Gravel was hauled in side-dump railroad cars from pits 70 miles west. The cars with the gravel were moved out onto the railroad trestles, from which the gravel was dumped into place.

Meanwhile, test drilling was performed nearby in search of just the right sort of clay material to form the impervious core of the dam. Suitable material was found both above and below the dam site. When the gravel toes were complete, timber cut in the reservoir area was used to build up trestles to support the pipes that would bring the dredged clay material and water to the "core pool," as the water body on the upper surface of the dam was called. The four dredges each had a rotary 7-foot cutter head that chewed up the native clay material, which was then pumped up the 28-inch pipelines to the dam. The mix was 15 percent clay, 85 percent water. This material came gushing at a high rate onto the dam. The dredged material was released near the crest of the dam under construction, and ran downhill into the core pool. The heavier material, such as sand, would precipitate out first, and by the time the water got to the core pool it contained only the very finest silt, which was the least permeable when settled and was ideal for the core of the dam. Draglines and other heavy equipment were used to move the settled material to form the body of the dam. The 12,500-horsepower pumping units on the barges could lift the slurry 250 feet. The dredges operated as much as 7 miles from the dam and dredged material from as far as 50 feet below the surface.

As notable as the technical achievements were, the social scene was even more interesting. As employment reached its peak at 10,456 jobs in 1936, 18 shantytowns with many forms of entertainment were in round-the-clock operation. Some of these, such as New Deal and Delano Heights, weren't much. The most substantial of them was Wheeler. With 3,500 residents, Wheeler had 65 businesses, a fair number of them saloons.

One of the main occupations in these establishments was taxi dancing. Women would dance with strangers, no matter how loutish and heavy-footed, if the men would buy them beer. The beer was 10 cents, and the management rebated 5 cents of this to the lady. If she could hold 60 beers she could make 3 bucks a night. The beer was watered down of course, but it must have made those ladies slosh nevertheless. A correspondent for *Life* magazine described the dancing style, saying that the taxi dancers "lope around with their fares."

Down in a coulee behind Wheeler was Ruby Smith's house of excellent repute. It was only one of the establishments of its kind in a whole village of same. Ruby Smith apparently was the first madam to get to Wheeler, and was the best known. She seems to have been a sort of acting mayor of her particular suburb, besides being its leading entrepreneur. When a visiting correspondent wanted a few words from the shady-lady contingent, Ruby always obliged. Publicity is publicity. Ernie Pyle, the famous newspaperman, wrote that this village had an unprintable name, and of course he didn't print it. "Everybody calls it that," he said. Keep reading and you will find out what it was.

Seeking eyewitnesses to the various events at Fort Peck Dam, I went to the Nemont retirement home in Glasgow where I met two men who worked on the dam, Christ Lund and Clarence Rasmussen. Mr. Lund, 88 years old when I visited, was born in Norway and followed his Viking blood to this country in 1921. On the dam project he worked as a fore-men of carpenters, and pulled down 65 cents an hour. At first he worked building forms for the concrete lining in the four 24-foot-diameter tunnels that would carry water from the reservoir to the power plants. Later, he worked building forms for the concrete spillway.

Christ lived in the Glasgow vicinity before the dam was built. He had an uncle near the town of Tampico, some distance out of Glasgow. He worked in farming, and at any other kind of work he could find. Before the dam, he said, "I hustled all the time, and there just wasn't any work."

Christ said most of the men in his crew were from Montana, and from all over Montana, "Kalispell, Jordan—all over." One of his main rec-ollections is how glad he and the other men were to have work, and how scared they were of losing it. "We didn't know the Depression was go-ing to be over. We thought when the dam work was finished, we'd be back like we were before. I had men tell me that if I would keep them working, I could sleep with their wives."

By 1937 most of the carpentry was finished and Christ drifted off to work elsewhere. Nevertheless, he has fond memories of the dam project. "Everything went twenty-four hours a day. The town never shut down. And the work. Ah, it was the noisiest work you ever heard. Blasting, and trains coming through all the time...."

Clarence Rasmussen also had memories of the dam. Clarence was born in 1912 in Baylor, Montana. "Bet you don't know where Baylor is," he said. Correct. Forty miles north of Glasgow. On the family homestead near Baylor, Clarence operated an acetylene plant that provided gas for lights. When the dam project got going, he was offered a job operating a hot-mix plant that used acetylene. This was for asphalt used in build-ing the new road from Glasgow to Fort Peck. The job paid 60 cents an hour.

Then he got an offer to "skin cat," dragging 80-foot lengths of sheet steel piling around the work site. "You could hear it for ten miles," he said. In the next few years, Clarence did a variety of jobs on the project, mostly operating heavy equipment.

He recalled that a lot of new equipment got its first major test at Fort Peck, and a lot of it didn't pass. The Ford-Marmon trucks flunked, for ex-ample. White and Diamond T trucks proved more reliable. Some of these trucks had an intriguing innovation: heaters in the cabs. They didn't last long, though. "Everybody stole them to put in their cars." Clarence stole one too. Put it in his new '34 Plymouth.

One of Clarence's jobs was helping put up the wooden trestle that supported the big pipes carrying the slurry from the dredges. Each set of trestle was good for another 20 feet of vertical distance, and when the fill reached the new level the trestle had to be dismantled and rebuilt at the new level. Cranes pulled the posts out, and the men reinserted them at the new level into holes that were made by a hose jet. The hose came from a hydraulic pump on a barge in the core pool.

The dredge lines had traps to catch trash picked up by the dredges, and Clarence recalled that some of the material it picked up was pretty interesting. "Hundreds of buffalo skulls, for one thing. Old guns. Parts of an old steamboat that had been wrecked."

One of Clarence's most vivid memories is from September 22, 1938. "I can see it in my mind right now exactly the way it was. I was operating a crane that day, moving pipe. All at once I started tipping the wrong way. I hit the ground running. I wasn't running fast, but I passed some guys that were. I was jumping cracks in the ground."

This was the big slide, when 5 million cubic yards of fill slid out into the lake. Eight men were killed, and six of the bodies were not found. The slide left doubt about whether the dam should be completed. A blue-ribbon panel eventually said it was okay, and the dam was completed on October 11, 1940. The slide had delayed completion by about a year.

According to the Corps of Engineers, the population of Tennessee could stand on Fort Peck Dam without excessive crowding. The dam is four miles long and contains 125.6 million cubic yards of fill. The dam probably didn't meet 1992 standards for public comment and minimum environmental impact. A hundred and five farms and ranches were flooded, and their owners were not consulted. Some of them complained.

By the time the dam was completed, the Depression was pretty well licked, and a really big money maker, World War II, was on the horizon. From there on, things went along differently. But between 1933 and 1940, the work on the dam was a life-saver for thousands of people. Any veteran of the project will tell you, "It was the greatest thing that ever happened on the Hi-Line."

Oh yeah, that suburb that Ruby Smith was mayor of? Clarence Rasmussen remembers it well. "They called it Peckerville. Everybody called it that."

GOVERNOR'S CUP WALLEYE TOURNAMENT

Fort Peck Dam was the mother of all pork barrels. When they built it, and for some years thereafter, they argued about what it was for. Flood control maybe, power generation, navigation? That all started back in the 1930s, the most no-fun decade in this century so far, so it is no great wonder that recreation didn't get mentioned much if at all.

In recent years, however, fishing and hunting in and around Fort Peck Reservoir have become important sources of income for nearby communities. Glasgow, a few miles up the road from the marina near the dam, is in a particularly good position to benefit. In recent years, Glasgow and the reservoir have received good publicity by the train-load as a result of fishing tournaments. One of these competitions, the Montana Governor's Cup Walleye Tournament was in its fifth year in 1992, and I decided to go and take a look at it.

I admit that I'm skeptical about the desirability of fishing for money. I have memories, from when I was a small boy, of the annual trout derby in the Yellowstone near Livingston. In that fandango, the derby officials selected a different section of river each year, and then hundreds if not thousands of participants showed up on derby day to flail the water in an effort to garner the prize of 1,000 silver dollars. It was not a pretty picture.

Two things the Governor's Cup Walleye Tournament had that the Livingston trout derby did not have are plenty of room and a limited number of participants. The maximum number of two-person teams allowed is 200, although that many never yet have showed up. In 1992, 103 teams participated. The area designated for the tournament consisted of the portion of the reservoir within 20 miles of the Fort Peck Marina.

The tournament rules were very specific about just about everything. Boats were allowed to leave the marina at 7 A.M. each day. On the first day in the 1992 tournament, the boats left in the order of the numbers they had been assigned; on the second day they left in reverse order. Each boat returned a slip with the boat's number to officials at the end of the fishing day to make sure nobody got stranded on the water.

The boats leave the marina at five-second intervals. Tournament Director Rob Hurly said that in other years officials had turned all the boats loose at once and created a dangerous situation as everybody scrambled to get out of the bay and head to their fishing spots.

Each team knows in advance where it will start fishing. Before the tournament, the participants spend at least one day "pre-fishing" the lake to find out where the fish are and what they are biting. Of course, by tournament day, the fish are not likely to be in the same spot but they should be nearby.

Mike Kohler, a professional walleye fisherman who helped run the Governor's Cup, said that pre-fishing is one of the keys to success in walleye tournaments. People who live nearby and fish the same lake for sport may actually have a disadvantage when it comes to tournament fishing, he said. Local fishermen think they know where the fish are, and may not take pre-fishing seriously. This gives the advantage to outsiders who come in and do the work necessary to locate fish. Local fishermen tend to "fish history," by fishing where they have found fish in the past, Kohler said.

Each fisherman in the tournament is allowed to operate two rods at a time. Boats have "live wells," which are tanks of water where fish are kept alive. Under the rules of the 1992 Governor's Cup, each boat was allowed to have no more than three fish in its live well at a time. When three are caught and placed in the live well, the boat must go to one of the 15 or 20 patrol boats that work the tournament to have the fish "weighed."

At the tournament in 1992, fish were not actually weighed, but measured. They were measured for length only, and a mathematical formula was then applied to determine the fish's weight. This method is not likely to give the exact weight of any fish, but when applied to a large number of fish it is likely to come out close to the actual average weight. Above all, this method of estimating weight minimizes the handling of fish, which normally are returned to the lake immediately after they are measured.

Anglers must keep fish if they are seriously injured and not likely to survive, and can keep them if they are over 24 inches long. Contestants caught over 400 fish in the tournament and only seven died, Hurly said. The biggest walleye caught was logged in as weighing 14.37 pounds as estimated by the weight estimation system, but when the fish was brought in and actually weighed it tipped the scales at only about 10.5 pounds. The angler was given credit for the 14.37 pounds under the rules. Kohler said the reason the fish weighed so much less than indicated by its length, over 30 inches, was that it was an old fish, and old fish lose flesh, just like old fishermen.

Each boat is allowed to register five fish each day. Anglers can "upgrade" by replacing smaller fish that they register early with larger ones that they catch later. As long as fish are returned to the water, there is no limit to the number that each boat is allowed to catch. The smallest fish that may be entered is a 14-incher, which is calculated to weigh one pound.

All the contestants in the Governor's Cup were required to be back into the marina by 3 P.M. At the end of the first day, the top total weight recorded by a boat was 36.33 pounds, an average of over 7 pounds per fish.

The first day of the tournament was followed by a fish fry at the campground below the dam. Rob Hurly said this is a popular event with people of the region, with lots of folks volunteering to help with the work. "I had 80 volunteers," he said. When we got down to the serious eating, it was a major case of man bite fish as we all went into a feeding frenzy and devoured 600 pounds of walleye, along with all the side dishes. Hurly said the fish is purchased in Canada.

Next morning the author was trying to sleep in the back of his truck at the marina when the big engines started roaring long before 6 A.M. as the contestants lined up to launch their boats. They all got into the water well before the 7 A.M. beginning of fishing, and spent the extra time idling in the water or tied up to a pier. Then came seven o'clock and the boats moved out single file to the registry boat near the mouth of the bay. Once they were registered and turned loose, they took off in sheets of spray.

When they came back that afternoon some of them were substantially richer. The North Dakota team that had the most poundage the first day came through again on the second to win the $5,870 first prize. Second prize, $3,036, went to a Glasgow team, and third place, $2,429, went to a team with a Glasgow man and a North Dakota man. Cash prizes were awarded for the top 11 finishers. Eleventh place took $405.

Of the 206 people participating, 45 were from Glasgow. The flat part of Montana generated 77 teams, North Dakota 15, Wyoming six, South Dakota and Canada two apiece, Oregon and Colorado one each. The entry fee per boat was $260. Eighty percent of the money taken in is paid out as prize money. Much of the remainder is donated to the Montana Department of Fish Wildlife and Parks to improve walleye habitat.

I asked Hurly if tournament fishing requires any equipment not used by ordinary recreational walleye fishermen. He said the contestants from Glasgow just used their usual equipment, and he thought everybody else did too. "Usual equipment" seemed to consist mostly of aluminum boats with outboard motors ranging from 80 to 150 horsepower, and small electric trolling motors, usually mounted on the front. Boats must have a live well, and they would be lost without their fish-finding sonar. A set of all this equipment runs from $12,000 upwards, I was told. Then you need a large car or pickup to pull the whole thing.

Equipment is getting more and more serious. Mike Kohler, the professional fisherman, said boat location devices using satellites are sometimes used to help boats fix locations so they can return to a spot later.

Everybody seemed to agree that the Governor's Cup was a good time. Several of the participants interviewed said the organization of the tournament and the quality of the fishing are both better than most other tournaments in other places. And not just for walleyes. One tournament fisherman brought in a 4-pound smallmouth bass, just to demonstrate that the reservoir contains other good species too. An Oregon fisherman was impressed with the friendliness of the people. "They wave at you," he said. "It's not like back in Oregon."

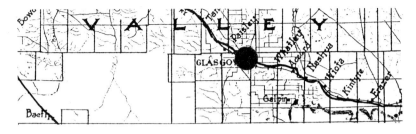

GLASGOW

Before Glasgow was Glasgow, it was railroad siding 45. This moniker did not exactly sing on the ear, so residents wanted a better name. Accommodating them, a railroad clerk in St. Paul spun his globe, stopped it with his finger, and where his finger stopped was Glasgow, Scotland. Siding 45 became Glasgow, Montana Territory. That was in 1887. By May 1888, the town had four tent saloons and a restaurant. Stores, houses, and all the other structures of civilization followed. Initially, most of the nearby land was Indian reservation, but in 1888, 18 million acres of this was thrown open to be grabbed by non-Indians. The country surrounding Glasgow quickly became sheep and cattle ranches and homesteads, which it largely remains today, with the changes brought by time.

One big event in the history of Glasgow was the nearby construction of Fort Peck Dam in the 1930s. Fort Peck helped to jog Glasgow out of the Depression, and this progress was further assisted by the construction north of town of an Air Force base. One book about Glasgow and its history is titled *From Buffalo Bones to Sonic Boom*. The buffalo bones were the ones that the first settlers found still on the ground after the great slaughter was over, and the sonic boom was the ultimate sign of local progress, the sound of the U.S. Air Force at work. At its peak, the base housed up to 10,000 people.

By and by, however, the base became obsolete, and was abandoned. Sonic booms went the way of buffalo bones. Nevertheless, you won't get any pessimism out of Doris Vallard, editor of the Glasgow *Courier*. "Glasgow is a prairie rose about to bloom," she said to me with a smile. "Suitors are at our door."

One of the suitors is a 1,200-unit retirement community that is being developed from the housing and facilities at the former Glasgow Air Force Base. North of Glasgow in the middle of this ultimate high plain sits the abandoned base. This is the standard Air Force Base with thousands of feet of runway, striped water towers, a school, gymnasium, hundreds of military style duplex and 4-plex houses, every American comfort for all the young bachelors and the young moms and dads and all their kids who came to Glasgow Air Force Base to wait for the apocalypse. To the casual observer, the base might seem like the king of all white elephants. But not to Pat Kelly, retired president of Valley Park Inc., owner of the housing portion of the base.

Kelly is a retired Air Force officer originally from Sidney, and loves everything about eastern Montana. "I have been all over the world. I liked the Far East, the Sun Belt…but eastern Montana is where I wanted to come home to. I missed the sunsets and sunrises, the deer and the antelope, and the subtlety of the landscape. Three of the last six years, we haven't even used the snowplow."

He knows that a lot of other people would like eastern Montana too if they knew about it. He's telling as many of them as he can. He tells them not only about how great eastern Montana is, but that for a nominal sum, they can retire there. Yes, the former Glasgow Air Force Base is now a retirement community for retired soldiers, sailors, fliers, and all the others. And also for anybody else who is interested. It's not Glasgow Air Force Base anymore either. Now it's the town of St. Marie, complete with its own post office and Zip Code.

A second suitor is the Boeing Corporation, which has purchased the runways at the former air base for testing its aircraft. "Boeing is mum on jobs," Vallard said, adding that there will be some jobs at least, although it may be a few years before they materialize.

Another major asset that holds promise for local development is Fort Peck Reservoir. "Every year we have five or six fishing tournaments," Vallard pointed out. "These tournaments bring writers and film crews that have given us nationwide exposure. Our fishing for lake trout, walleye, and chinook salmon is known throughout the U.S. and Canada."

Other types of tourism and recreation also contribute to the county coffers, Vallard said. For example, a couple of people from New York are organizing ranch vacations, where city people can visit working ranches and participate in the ranch work if they want to. Also, she said, more and more visitors come to the area from western Montana, where development has closed off much hunting and fishing. Every little bit helps, and there are various bits and pieces to the recreational picture.

Vallard said the Conservation Reserve Program has hurt local implement dealers to some extent, but this has been partly offset by Canadians coming down to buy tractors and other farm machinery.

Canadians come down for other reasons too. "We have a big influx of Canadians on the weekends," she said. "They come down from Regina to take advantage of our low prices." One of the popular attractions for Canadians is garage sales, Vallard said.

There also is some northbound traffic across the Canadian border. "We have an international airport," Vallard said. "People from all over the country stop here on their way up to fish in Canada."

Despite all the suitors for the budding prairie rose, Glasgow faces some uncertainties too. What would happen, for example, if a Wal-Mart or a Shopko were to locate in town? At present, people from Glasgow sometimes drive to Williston to go to Wal-Mart, Vallard said, adding that the five- or ten-year survival of existing small businesses could be threatened if a discount store were to locate in Glasgow. Not that there is any immediate threat of such a development. If Boeing were to employ a sizeable number of people, it might make some discount store consider coming, she said. "New development in Glasgow is going to depend on Boeing, but the basis of our existence continues to be agriculture," she said. And of course agriculture is an uncertain business. Besides the usual problems, Vallard said ranchers are worried about the possible introduction of black-footed ferrets into the nearby C.M. Russell Wildlife Refuge. If the ferrets were to spread, she said, they could interfere with the management of prairie dogs, and with ranching operations.

None of these worries is enough to take the bloom off the rose, however. No doubt Glasgow, Montana will be around as long as Glasgow, Scotland, even if some of the suitors decide to bolt.

THE SLEEPING BUFFALO RESORT

Beside Highway 2 between Saco and Malta, there is a roadside shrine containing the sleeping buffalo rocks. These two rocks, which resemble sleeping buffalo, are lodged in a wooden shelter. The story is that a band of Indians at the desperate edge of starvation was wandering in the vicinity and mistook the rocks (at their original location some miles away) for buffalo. As they approached the rocks, however, they discovered real buffalo beyond the rocks, and the band was saved. Since then, the rocks reportedly have been sacred to some Indians. Local residents say that Indians passing by in cars sometimes still stop to pay their respects.

The sleeping buffalo shrine also marks the entrance to the Sleeping Buffalo Resort, long a landmark on the Hi-Line. The Sleeping Buffalo had its beginning in 1922 when a wildcat oil driller struck a tremendous flow of hot water 3,200 feet below the surface. In 1992 this artesian water was still flowing: 1,700 gallons per minute with a shut-off pressure of about 500 pounds per square inch.

At first the hot water was used only by cowboys for their weekly bath, but during the 1930s the federal Works Projects Administration built up the facilities and the "Saco Health Plunge" became a prominent recreational facility.

Bad luck came in 1957 when the well quit flowing. A replacement well drilled the following year was destroyed in 1959 when the ground shifted as a result of the Yellowstone earthquake. A new well was drilled and the resort continued to operate most of the time, although there was a series of owners and one two-year closure. When I visited in 1992, the place was owned by Doug Plouffe and Roger Ereaux. Mr. Plouffe showed me around and explained the operation to me.

"I'm just a dumb farmer myself," Plouffe said. "Roger is the one who has the vision you need for a place like this." For example, Plouffe said, at one point some other people held shares in the resort, and they decided that expenses were getting out of hand. Ereaux was trying to talk them into building a picnic area. Finally after being firmly told, "No," Ereaux seemed to agree to forgo the picnic area. Actually, Ereaux had no patience with such short-sightedness. "Next thing we knew," Plouffe said, "there were the concrete trucks backing up to fill the forms for the picnic area. And you know, it's been one of the best things we have. People love it. Roger knew that. He has the vision."

The popularity of the picnic area is easy to understand. It is a shady, grassy area out of the wind. Best of all, it has a clear view of the 60-by-120-foot outside pool, the waterslide that leads into it, and a wading pool off to one side. Anyone who has ever wanted to relax in the shade while being able to keep an eye on their kids of various ages wearing themselves to an absolute frazzle in the sun and water would appreciate the place.

The outside pool, which has a temperature range of 78° to 80°, is only one of the three pools at the Sleeping Buffalo. One indoor pool is 50 by 60 feet, with a temperature of 94°. An 8-by-20-foot hot pool operates at 106 degrees, which is the temperature of unmixed water direct from the well. Other facilities include a restaurant, a small grocery store, laundromat, 36 motel rooms, 78 RV hookups, and an "unlimited camping area." A large new facility is the "Buffalo Barn," which contains a bar, dining room, meeting room, and dance floor.

The Buffalo Barn is new because the old Buffalo Barn burned down in 1988. The new barn was dedicated in proper style in 1991 when professional daredevil Robbie Knievel jumped his motorcycle over it. "He almost missed his landing ramp," Plouffe said. "We had a semi flatbed tilted up for him to land on, but of course he couldn't see it until he was in midair over the barn, and he almost missed it. But he didn't." Knievel returned in 1992, and he and his flying cycle cleared an entire wagon train.

Plouffe said the barn is vital to the operation of "The Buffalo," as everybody calls it thereabout. "It's the only place you can put three hundred people if it starts to rain," he said. Also, the barn is used by all sorts of acts that come to perform. A lot of these performers are well-known country western singers. "We had the Garrett Brothers, Ferlin Husky, and lots of others."

Country western music is not the only attraction at the barn, which seems to have unlimited variety in its activities. For example, there are the oil wrestlers. The oil wrestlers, Plouffe explained, are young women wearing mainly a thin coat of oil who accept bids from members of the audience to wrestle with them. Audience participation also includes applying the coat of oil. Not everybody approved of the oil wrestling. "We lost some business over it," Plouffe said. The wrestlers themselves were not complaining, however.

"They came up from Billings," Plouffe said. "I guess they were surprised at how many of these old cowboys up here wanted to oil them. They wanted to come right back for another performance, but we said, 'Maybe once a year'."

Another popular performer at the barn was the evangelist Lowell Lundstrom, famous for the "Lundstrom Crusade" on television, who also packed the place.

Approaching Wolf Point from the east.

Above: *The Daniels County Courthouse in Scobey, and that of Sheridan County in Plentywood are a study in Hi-Line styles.*
Facing page, top: *Ready for emergencies on a quiet day in Culbertson.*
Bottom: *A summer storm approaching Flaxville demonstrates the wind's primacy along the Hi-Line.*

iii

Top: Grain-field geometry at Peerless. *Above:* A & S Tribal Industries at Poplar, Montana's largest manufacturing plant. *Right:* Poplar-area travelers' landmark.

Above: *Wolf Point grain elevators.* ***Left:*** *Waterslide and outdoor pool at Sleeping Buffalo Resort, where hot springs flow at 1,700 gallons per minute.*

Facing page, top: Aerial view of base of Fort Peck Dam from 5,000 feet, June 1935. From foreground to background can be seen Missouri River Bridge and approaches with ground dumped for downstream toe of dam. ***Bottom:*** Destruction wrought by the September 1938 landslide of 5 million cubic yard of fill that killed eight men. (US Army Corps of Engineers photos)
Above: Powerhouse at Fort Peck Dam.

Above: A day of competition begins at the Governor's Cup Walleye Tournament, Glasgow. *Right:* The proposed retirement community of St. Marie, formerly family housing at Glasgow Air Force Base. *Below:* Railroad stations and European names: the Hi-Line's legacy of its founding.

Above: *In Chinook, the Blaine County Museum includes a reproduction of the office of Lloyd Sweet, a one-time resident who endowed a healthy scholarship fund for graduates of Chinook High School.*
Top: *Mike Perry, publisher of the Chinook and Harlem papers, in front of his offices in Harlem.*

As the local
slogan claims,
Havre Has It!
Above: *Northern
Montana College.*
Right: *A 450-
horsepower Big
Bud tractor's
tilting cab offers
easy access to
components.*
Below: *Frank
Derosa in the
underground
tunnels he's
developing into
"Havre Beneath
the Streets."*

Left: Welcome to Chester.
Below: Shelby's City Hall displays Art Moderne flair.
Bottom: The vast arena for the Dempsey-Gibbons prize fight at Shelby in 1923 covered six acres, held 40,000 seats, and used 1.25 million feet of lumber. (Montana Historical Society Photo)

Above: The Oil Patch
is half of the bars in
Kevin.
Right: The author's
tutors in oil patch
history at Kevin were,
left to right: Dan
Mitchell, Connie Huso,
Henry Sieben, Marian
Irgens.

Left: Little Flower Parish in Browning.
Below: Leo Wolverine on the job at Browning's Blackfeet Writing Company.

Hi-Line images mix boosterism and humor, including a "Tinman" near Glasgow, hay-bale figure south of Scobey, the Coca-Cola sign in Joplin, customized grain bins outside Medicine Lake, and the farmer's eternal prayer north of Malta.

Cut Bank's 27-foot talking penguin highlights the town's visitor center.

The barn has an oversized dance floor, which Plouffe said is another example of Ereaux's vision. "When they put the dance floor in, I thought it was too big. I told Roger, 'We're never going to need a dance floor that big.' Then we got some Canadian fiddlers down here and they packed that dance floor so tight that nobody could move. We made it even bigger after that."

The word "potential" comes up again and again in discussing the Sleeping Buffalo Resort with its owners. They are almost overcome by the potential of the place. Ereaux told me, "This is one of the finest mineral hot springs in the country. We'd like to turn it into another Fairmont, if we could get financing," referring to the fancied-up pool and resort near Anaconda.

The year before the fire burned the Buffalo Barn, the resort did $450,000 in business, Ereaux said. The two years after that, business fell off to $425,000. In 1991, business was $650,000, with $700,000 expected for 1992. "If we had new rooms adjoining the pool, we could get our business up over two million dollars. The potential is endless. We could put in a casino. We could use the hot water to operate greenhouses and put twenty or twenty-five people to work. Right now we are looking at using some of the heat from our water to generate electricity. This would be helpful, because we pay $2,000 to $2,500 a month for electricity.

"We've got everything right here within one square mile," Ereaux said. "I challenge anybody to show me a square mile with more recreation than we have right here." Publicity material provided by the resort indicates that activities include, in part, golf, volleyball, softball, horseshoes, cards, dancing, water skiing, fishing, hunting, motocross races, dog races, roping, horse races, car races, chariot races, hide races [in which horseback competitors drag passengers on cowhides], demolition derbies, snowmobiling, ice skating, ice fishing, cross-country skiing, bird watching, and rodeos. Or combinations thereof. One interesting sort of contest at the Buffalo is the "Rope and Stroke," in which teams first compete at roping steers at the rodeo arena right next door, and then move over to the resort's eight-hole golf course for the second part of the competition. Most of the hunting and fishing takes place at Nelson Reservoir, a mile or so away.

Ereaux and Plouffe said people come from all over to the Buffalo. "We have a lot of people from eastern Montana, Sidney, Wolf Point, and a lot of Canadian trade. On Victoria Day, you can't get near the place, with all the Canadians that come. People come from Wyoming, North Dakota. We are a low-income tourist attraction. You can stay here for half what it costs at Fairmont. Our rooms are not up to Fairmont's standards, but everything else we have is better. In Canada, they want eighty dollars a night for a motel room."

People along the Hi-Line make good use of the Buffalo. For the dispersed Hi-Line families that have scattered in every direction, it is the place to get back together and celebrate. "Every weekend from Memorial Day until the end of September we have family reunions booked,"

Plouffe said. The Buffalo Barn has a fine dining room which is popular for wedding receptions.

As Ereaux points out, for people coming from the east, the Buffalo is the first recreational facility along Highway 2. It needs to be developed, he said. "The potential is terrific."

MALTA

The story of how Malta got its name is the same as how Glasgow got its name. When the railroad arrived in 1887, the siding where Malta is now was designated as siding 54. Citizens appealed to the railroad, a blindfolded clerk in St. Paul spun the globe, stopped it with his finger, and the town of Malta had its name. The first non-Indian resident of the site was a bone merchant who recruited Indians to help him pick up buffalo bones, which he piled in huge stacks along the railroad track until they could be shipped east. In the years since the passing of the buffalo bones, farming, ranching and, more lately, mining have contributed to the local economy.

Curtis Starr is the editor of the *Phillips County News* in Malta. I interviewed him in his office early in 1992. "So how is Malta doing?" I asked.

"We're doing better than Chinook," he said emphatically. "Our business section is better than theirs." He explained that he had co-owned the paper in Chinook when he first came to the state from Utah and so was familiar with that town's situation. He has owned the Malta paper since 1985.

Better than Chinook is not necessarily that good, however. "Nobody's turning cartwheels over how well we are doing," he said. "We have a substantial economic base in cattle-raising, and last year was good for wheat. This year there is a lot of nervous laughter by merchants and farmers as they watch the weather.

"The mine [Pegasus gold mine in the nearby Little Rocky Mountains] employs 200 people and has kept us stable for the last 10 years or so. A lot of Canadians come through on their way to Great Falls or Billings." He said he sympathizes with the small Canadian communities that get by-passed by Canadians on their way south to the lower prices in the U.S. Of course there is no guarantee that the Canadian traffic will continue. The Canadian dollar is getting stronger, Starr noted, and Canada is talking about collecting a tax on Canadians returning from shopping trips to the States.

Although the three-hour drive from Malta to Great Falls or Billings is not enough to stop Canadians, it is enough to stop most local retail business from leaving Malta, Starr said. "That's one way we're better off than Chinook. Chinook is a lot closer to Great Falls, and a lot of Chinook people go to Great Falls to shop."

In many ways, Starr said, Malta is typical of a lot of other small towns in eastern Montana. "There is a sense of discouragement. There is distrust of the federal government. We know a lot of people want to turn us into a pasture for buffalo and prairie dogs. But farmers are always hopeful. And in town we have a lot of mom-and-pop stores. These folks can't afford to hire any help, and if the owners are not there, the doors are closed. We are lucky to have a lot of young store owners. People take responsibility for the community. We usually have 35 or 40 people at our Chamber of Commerce meetings, compared to about 10 in the communities east or west of us. We are typical in that we have economic development groups trying to do one thing or another, rather than sitting on their hands and waiting for fate. Malta has the usual small-town hassle getting and keeping doctors. "Right now we have two doctors and a doctor's assistant."

As the summer of 1992 continued, the rains did not come and did not come to the Malta area, and the nervous laughter Starr mentioned turned into a grim resignation. Then the rain did come, mostly too late and too little. "Maybe next year," some said. That's why they call it "next-year country."

KID CURRY

Some thoughtful soul has noted that if a person has one watch, he or she will know what time it is. If a person has two watches, then he or she will have a controversy. Having more than one watch is like trying to reconstruct historical events that have more than one point of view. The story of Kid Curry is such a case. The record is full of positively stated facts by impeccable witnesses. The trouble is, there is hardly a one of these facts that does not conflict directly with some other equally well-founded fact. Having warned of possible ambiguities, I hereby state the following.

The Montana Historical Society has no file on Kid Curry. That's because his name was really Harvey Logan. Harvey is believed to have showed up in the Little Rockies in 1884, accompanied by one of his brothers, Hank. Later he was joined by his other brothers, Johnnie and "Lonine," shown in the record as Lonnie, Lonny, Lownie, or Loney.

The record makes it clear that the Logan boys were born in Kentucky, unless it was Virginia or Illinois, and were raised by an aunt in Missouri, or maybe Kansas. The Kid was said to have taken the name "Curry" because of his admiration for Flat-Nosed George Curry, a prominent holdup man and rustler in Wyoming who apparently had taken the Logans under his wing and taught them a trade.

One source said that the Kid and Hank came to Montana from Pueblo, Colorado, where they had "had some trouble." Another authority agrees that they came from Pueblo, and adds that they followed a cattle stampede all the way from Pueblo to Montana, with a posse close behind.

At any rate, they showed up in the Little Rockies in 1884, and began working for cattle ranches there. Partisans of the Curry boys said that all of them were well-liked, though another source said that the Kid was "morose when sober and bitter when drunk." He was said to have a "sour disposition." Pinkerton detectives, who may have been prejudiced, later said the Kid had "not one good point." They said he "drinks heavily and has bad habits." This was all referring to the Kid's later tendencies, though there is no doubt he had been somewhat that way right along.

We have one heart-warming account of how at least one of the Curry boys felt bad about being illiterate, and an old-timer, "Dad" Marsh, storekeeper in Landusky, obtained reading primers and patiently taught the lad his ABCs. This came in handy later when the Currys unexpectedly got into the forgery business.

From his arrival in 1884 until 1894, the Kid seems to have gotten along all right with his neighbors, even if he was not a model citizen. Some accounts say the Kid even got along okay with a local character named Pike Landusky; others say he didn't. The ones who say he didn't give various possible reasons. One says Pike borrowed a plow, broke it, and gave it back without fixing it. Some suggest the whole problem was that Lonnie was paying too much attention to one of Pike's stepdaughters. *Somebody* was paying attention to her, and she gave birth to a fine boy, which was named either Harvey or Lonnie, according to the records. The new mother's name was Elfie, unless it was Elsie, or maybe Effie.

Late in 1894, Lonnie and the Kid were accused of cattle rustling. One of the accusers was Pike Landusky. The two were arrested and turned over to the local deputy sheriff, Pike Landusky. Pike didn't have a jail, so he chained them to a log. Then, according to some mild accounts, he abused them, both physically and verbally. Another account provided by a friend of the Curry family holds that "Pike worked them over until their faces looked like chopped meat. He stomped on them and kicked them around until he got tired." Then he took them to Fort Benton, where they paid a $50 fine and were released.

Meanwhile back in the town of Landusky, it was Christmas, and Pike and some of the boys had ordered up a whopping mess of oysters and recruited one of the better range cooks to make as much oyster stew as everybody could eat. This feast went on for three days. On the 27th, Pike was standing in Jew Jake's place when the Kid and a couple of his pals drifted in. The Kid immediately lit into Pike, got him down and pounded his face to a pulp. Then he let him up. Pike reached into his coat. Partisans of Mr. Landusky thought he was reaching for a handkerchief to wipe his bloody nose with. Others said he reached for his gun. Some said he pulled out his gun and attempted to fire at the Kid, but it was a new gun and Pike hadn't got the safety mechanism figured out yet. At any rate the Kid pulled his own gun and shot Pike: 1. once in the head; 2. twice in the head; 3. once in the body; or 4. twice in the body. It was all the same to Pike, who was quickly dead. The Kid then took it on the lam. Most citizens felt that the shooting was self defense and that the kid could have beat the rap. Somebody apparently suggested this to the Kid, and he said it was too easy for justice to go astray.

Some accounts suggest that up until the shooting of Landusky, the Kid was just a sort of over-aged juvenile delinquent, victim of a disadvantaged home environment. These accounts imply that the trauma of gunning Landusky down in self defense so traumatized the Kid that he snapped, became disillusioned, decided to give up honest cattle ranching, and partly honest cattle ranching, and to hit the owlhoot trail in dead earnest. So that's what he did.

The Pinkerton Detective Agency took a serious interest in the Kid's career, and kept a box score of his known accomplishments. According to this source, the Kid killed three sheriffs in three different states, killed one deputy sheriff, wounded three deputies, killed five civilians, escaped from two jails, held up three trains and at least one bank.

The Kid's most famous deed in Montana was the holdup of the Great Northern passenger train #3 outside of Malta on July 3, 1901. There is variance in the theories of who the holdup men were, although Kid Curry was one, Harry Alonzo Longabaugh the second, and the third was one Camilla Hanks. Probably it was only Wanted posters that referred to Camilla Hanks as Camilla Hanks. To everybody else he was "Deaf Charlie."

Deaf Charlie had just been released from the prison in Deer Lodge for having held up a train near Big Timber 10 years earlier. In a newspaper photograph with his short prison haircut, Charlie looks like a malevolent version of Curly of the Three Stooges.

Records show that two men, one of them the Kid, got on the westbound train in Malta. Longabaugh got on as a regular passenger, and the Kid crawled onto a baggage car. Longabaugh may or may not have been a valuable assistant, because he reportedly had robbed the same train 10 years earlier, netting a mere $22 because he couldn't get the safe open.

When the train got out of town a ways, the Kid crawled over the tender and ordered the engineer to stop, which he did. Two other men then rode from under a bridge. Instructions were passed for everybody to stay in the train, and the two men from under the bridge began firing rifles close along the sides of the cars, which caused a quick cessation of all rubbernecking. The sheriff of Valley County was on the train, but he didn't feel lucky enough to take on the Curry boys by himself that day.

The Kid and Longabaugh uncoupled the baggage car and moved

if off some distance, before putting a stout charge of dynamite on top of the safe. The idea was that the dynamite would warp the safe and spring the door open. But it didn't. A second charge also failed. The gang needed more help, and they pressed the fireman into service. Maybe he was the one who suggested putting a lot of heavy iron on top of the charge for the third blast. At any rate, it worked. The loot consisted of unsigned currency in the amount of: 1. $88,000, 2. $65,000, 3. $50,000, or 4. $40,000, along with a box of watches and three bags of silver dollars.

One account said the fireman was such good help to the gang that they gave him one of the watches in gratitude. The fireman himself said he was pressed into service against his will, and although the Kid promised to give him one of the watches, he never did.

The watches were in a dilapidated condition because of the dynamite blasts, and the silver dollars were all cup-shaped from the force of the charges. Within a couple of days some of these concave coins were ringing on the counters of saloons in Great Falls.

By one account, at least three posses were got up to pursue the Kid. A participant in one of the posses said his group rode out of town until they found a big flat rock suitable for playing cards, which they did for three days before returning and reporting no sign of the criminals.

The unsigned currency turned out to be a great plague. The Kid and some of his helpers tried their hands at autographing it themselves, but the banks had the numbers and the Pinkertons were hot on the trail of anybody who passed one of the bills.

The Kid got arrested in Tennessee with some of the money in his possession, and was sentenced to 135 years in jail for various acts, including forgery and shooting a few policemen. While he was in a county jail awaiting transfer to state prison, he escaped. Unbiased observers noted that one of the Kid's business partners in Montana had recently sold a herd of horses for a large sum of money. It was further noted that someone from Montana had visited the kid shortly before his break.

Everyone agreed it must have been humiliating for the sheriff to have Kid Curry escape and ride away on the sheriff's best horse, but they thought maybe he could endure it better if he had the price of a Montana horse herd in his pocket.

The next reported sighting of the Kid was near Parachute, Colorado, after a botched train robbery. A deputy wounded one of the outlaws, who then committed suicide. The Pinkertons looked at the body and decided it was Kid Curry. In fact, they were sure of it. All their years of chasing him had paid off.

A little later, a bank was robbed nearby. One of the participants sounded a lot like Kid Curry. The Pinkertons dug up their body, looked at it again, photographed the bullet scars, sent the pictures around to people who knew the Kid. They all agreed it was the Kid.

However, the Kid's old pals, Longabaugh, a.k.a. the Sundance Kid, and George Parker, a.k.a. Butch Cassidy, were in South America. There were reports that the Kid was down there too. Although the Pinkertons had declared the Kid to be dead, George Pinkerton of that agency said that the Kid, along with his old companions, had bought a cattle ranch in Argentina, "on a high piece of table land from which they command a view of 25 miles in various directions, making their capture practically impossible."

The Kid was pretty active for a dead man. He visited Montana at least once, sent post cards from South America to various acquaintances, occasionally corresponded with newspaper reporters, and some citizens from the Little Rockies claimed to have made the trip down to visit him.

In 1910, newspapers reported that the Kid and his gang were forcing the government of South American republics to pay tribute, and these governments wanted the U.S. to help get rid of him.

In 1914 the Pinkertons tried to recruit one of the Kid's old acquaintances to go to South America to identify somebody they thought might be him. The man wouldn't go.

Every once in a while over the years, there were reports on the Kid, but never anything definite. As late as 1962, Sheriff Middlemas of Lewis and Clark County heard that a cantankerous old codger in California was letting it slip that in his younger days he was known as Kid Curry, and he had better not be messed with. The sheriff made inquiry and found that there were two 88-year-olds in Montana who could positively identify the Kid, which wasn't surprising considering all the times he had been identified previously. Middlemas went to California on some other business and checked on the Curry rumor. He came away convinced that the old guy was much too young to be the Kid, who probably was about 95 by that time. And then in 1973 came word from Alaska that an old-timer had died, and he had bullet scars matching those of the Kid. But since then, nothing.

The record does show that Pike Landusky's stepdaughter, former sweetheart of one or more of the Curry boys, the mother of little Lonnie, or little Harvey, returned to the Little Rockies for a visit in 1957. Nobody thought to ask her if her name was Elfie, or Elsie, or maybe Effie.

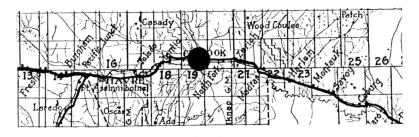

CHINOOK

The history of the town of Chinook began with the arrival of the railroad. At first it was named Dawes, after a local resident, but a newspaperman decided to honor the winds that melted valley snows in the winter and changed the town's name to Chinook. Like the rest of the Hi-Line country, the Chinook area was grazing land until the railroad came. After that came a considerable variety of activity, including sugar-beet farming and oil and gas development. A newspaper article in 1925 said that Chinook was "the capital of the sugar beet country of the north." In 1992, the "million dollar beet sugar factory" that figured prominently in the 1925 article sits abandoned outside of town, a concrete billboard for graffiti. About all that remains of the sugar-beet industry is the name of the Chinook sports teams: the Sugarbeeters. Cheerleaders have trouble working such a long name into their cheers, and newspaper editors have a hard time getting it into the headlines, so the teams are always known as the "Beeters."

One unusual thing about Chinook is that it had a wealthy financial benefactor that almost no one in the community ever met. This was Lloyd Sweet, who lived for a time in Chinook as a young man, then left, made a fortune, and gave part of it to Chinook. A scholarship fund that he created for graduates of Chinook High School is up to about $2.2 million, according to Ellen Solem, a Chinook accountant who is Financial Director for the fund. When Sweet died in 1989, he left about a million dollars to the town, of which $675,000 went to the scholarship fund and the remainder to the Sweet Nursing Home and the Chinook City Park Board. Sweet originally financed construction, remodeling, and expansion of the nursing home. He also donated substantial funds for maintenance of the city park, the land for which was donated by his mother in 1926. The interest from the scholarship fund provides about $170,000 per year for scholarships.

Solem said that the only restriction on the scholarships is that the recipients must be graduates of Chinook High School. "Theoretically, it could be somebody who graduated 40 years ago." She said Sweet insisted that the awards be made on merit, rather than need. She said that about

100 graduating seniors apply each year, of whom 15 or 20 get scholarships. The largest scholarships are $3,000, then $2,700, $2,100, $1,800, and $1,525. Many alumni who are in college apply, and the awards can be used to pursue advanced degrees if desired.

"It's a wonderful situation," Solem said. Several years ago, NBC News did a news story on the Sweet awards, and Solem said the administrators of the funds were flooded with calls from accountants and lawyers who had clients wanting to set up similar programs. "So this one man had a ripple effect that went far beyond Chinook," she said.

Sweet was born in the Wild West village of Ubet, and lived for a while in the Bears Paw Mountains, then went to Stanford University where he was graduated in economics in 1913. Apparently, he returned to Chinook after graduation; some reports indicate he was involved with a flour mill. He joined the Navy and left Chinook in 1918, never to return.

After discharge from the Navy, Sweet went to California where he made money at a variety of businesses and invested heavily in the stock market.

Sweet was 98 years old when he died. The executor of his estate said Sweet "made money at everything he did, spent relatively little of it, and kept at it for many years." The Blaine County Museum in Chinook contains a reproduction of Sweet's office. One wall has a strip chart showing long-term trends of the stock market.

Mike Perry is the editor of the Chinook *Opinion*. "Chinook," he told me, "is a community that tries hard. All through the years, through drought, low farm prices, people kept trying."

Perry said the centennial celebration in 1989 brought a high level of cooperation to the community, and this has persisted in the time since. "We are in a transition to more people being involved in the community. For example, we have eight people running for two seats on the school board. We have a lot of people who do a lot for the community, some who do little, and a few who won't do anything."

Perry said new ideas are rising in the community. For example, a new program is bringing more recreational opportunities to town, offering lessons in golf and tennis, and adult softball. These new developments are part of an evolutionary process, Perry said. Chinook is even experiencing a little growth in population, which is rare along the Hi-Line. Two new houses are being built in town, the first in quite a few years.

To sum up, Perry said Chinook is a low-key sort of place with all the small-town amenities. "We have a good school system, we have a doctor, churches, some of the best people in the world. Everything is right here."

THE BEARS PAW BATTLEFIELD

When you have seen one battlefield, you have not seen them all. Most Montanans have visited the Little Bighorn Battlefield; fewer have visited the Bears Paw Battlefield, just south of Chinook.

At the Bears Paw Battlefield, no marble monuments have been placed by a grateful nation, there is no visitor center with air-conditioned restrooms, no multi-media presentation. There are privies provided by the State of Montana, and some big boulders with plaques on them, placed by the Daughters of the American Revolution and others, and official government signs give a brief synopsis of events. Late in 1992, Congress approved and President George Bush signed legislation to make the Bears Paw Battlefield part of the multi-state, multi-site Nez Perce National Historical Park. Funding was not provided at that time.

On the battlefield itself, steel pegs indicate the location of Indian lodges, the spots where some individual Indians fell, breastworks and rifle pits manned by the Indians, and other features. Marking the sites was a low-budget undertaking, the effort primarily of one man: Charles Noyes. Noyes was a history enthusiast, and for a period, Blaine County surveyor. In 1928 the Chinook Lions Club and a Nebraska historian paid to bring several Nez Perce veterans to the battlefield to show where various events had happened.

Because there were survivors on both sides, events could be reconstructed. The feeling that comes through, as contrasted to the Little Bighorn Battlefield, reflects the Indian point of view. It is not hard to imagine how it must have felt to huddle in rifle pits along the creek while bullets and cannon shells smacked into the ground. The soldiers had their story too, and one is left to contemplate a large pit that served as a mass grave for the dead.

Other than that, there is mostly just the wind that slips down off the Bears Paws and stirs the grass. This is not a feel-good place. Instead, it is perhaps a place for meditation upon portions of the national heritage that do us shame. May we outgrow them.

In Chinook, a few miles north, the Blaine County Museum tells the story well. In 1877 peaceful Nez Perce in the Wallowa Valley of Oregon, friends to white people since the days of Lewis and Clark, were faced with removal from their land. Of the 4,000 Nez Perce existing at the time, 750 were non-treaty. Most of the treaty Indians lived on the Lapwai Reservation in Idaho. The government, under pressure from settlers, ordered the non-treaty Nez Perce to the Lapwai Reservation. After long dispute and encroachment by whites, some young Nez Perce men killed some white men who had abused the Indian people.

These killings caused a panic among white settlers, politics got going, nearby units of the U.S. Army mobilized, and the bands of non-treaty Nez Perce began their long march. Several chiefs were among them, including Joseph, who afterwards got the credit for setting strategy during

75

the Indians' fighting retreat to the Bears Paw, through he was not the war chief.

The intention of the Nez Perce was to temporarily quit the neighborhood where everybody was against them, cross the mountains and live with or near the Crow until the trouble blew over. Then they would return to Oregon. If they couldn't live with the Crow, they could continue on to Canada, a country ruled by a woman, Queen Victoria, and ostensibly an easier place to get along.

About 750 Nez Perce left Idaho, where the fighting had erupted. The entourage included women, children, old and sick people, and a horse herd numbering at least 2,000. They set out on July 16. Between then and October 4, when they surrendered, they were involved in 18 engagements, including four hot skirmishes and four major battles, winning or drawing all but the last.

After the battle, the Nez Perce captives totaled 418, including 87 men, 184 women, and 147 children. Those captured included an old man who was the son of Captain William Clark, the "Clark" of Lewis and Clark, and the old man's daughter and granddaughter.

Some critics have suggested that the Nez Perce thought they were in Canada when they camped where the soldiers found them. In truth, they knew perfectly well where they were. They stayed at the camp longer than they should have because many of them were exhausted, and they knew their chief pursuer, General O.O. Howard—"General Day After Tomorrow" they called him—was well behind. They didn't know that other troops had been summoned from Fort Keogh, where Miles City is now.

Nelson A. Miles, commander at Fort Keogh, caught up with the Nez Perce on September 30, and immediately ordered a charge. The Indians were not caught totally by surprise, and when the cavalrymen charged from the south, the Nez Perce sharpshooters were ready for them. They aimed at the leaders, the officers and non-commissioned officers, whose uniforms clearly showed their rank. Army casualties during the battle included 23 men killed, including two officers and seven sergeants. The Army troops included units of the Seventh Cavalry, with many veterans of the fight on the Little Bighorn. These men were said to be hungry for revenge against Indians, any Indians.

The Army captured or stampeded most of the Nez Perce horses at the beginning of the battle, to prevent any escape. Nevertheless, between the onset of the battle and October 8 when the prisoners were marched off, 233 Nez Perce including 140 men and boys and 93 women and girls escaped to the north. Some were captured by soldiers a day or two later, some were killed by Gros Ventre or Assiniboine, but most made it to Canada to join Sitting Bull. The wily old Sioux chief welcomed the Nez Perce, even though they were old enemies of the Sioux. He considered them fellow victims of the Americans.

The Nez Perce who arrived at the Sioux camp were in desperate condition, half-frozen and starved, many with multiple wounds. One man had cut off both his own feet and one hand to escape from manacles and leg irons.

The first Nez Perce who arrived at Sitting Bull's camp asked him to send warriors to help fight the soldiers. Some accounts indicate that a large Sioux war party was started south, but that it met survivors of the battle who told them of the surrender. It is interesting to think how the battle might have come out had the Sioux arrived in the nick of time for a return engagement with the Seventh Cavalry, but the ultimate result would not have been much better.

Immediately following the surrender, there was a strange scene of American soldiers fraternizing with the defeated Indians, showing friendship and respect. Even as the 23 dead soldiers were lying in their mass grave and with the Nez Perce dead still covered with snow on the battlefield, soldiers built huge fires for the Indians and gave them food and blankets. This behavior by troops who had been firing a cannon at a village composed mostly of women and children seems odd today. It was almost as though the war were a sporting event, and the Nez Perce had lost, although they were ahead in scoring right up to the last moment.

Surely, the Indians were in a pathetic condition. Assuredly, they had made monkeys out of the U.S. Army. O.O. Howard, General Day After Tomorrow, narrowly avoided being the only U.S. Army commander ever to have his own cannon fired against him by Indians. At the Battle of the Big Hole back in August, Nez Perce captured Howard's howitzer, but unfortunately they removed its wheels and rolled them down the mountainside minutes before the arrival of some Nez Perce who knew how to fire the gun.

The Nez Perce did no scalping, for which the soldiers were grateful. During the siege at the Bears Paw Battle, Indians gave water to wounded soldiers who were out of reach of their own men. All white men from Lewis and Clark on had noted the remarkable humanity of the Nez Perce. Although the Nez Perce had long been gifted with missionaries, the Christians had nothing to teach them about decency. The Nez Perce had their own strong notions of right and wrong, which was what led them to bridle at the treatment accorded them in the first place. So the soldiers building those fires and passing out the blankets probably had a sense of respect. Newspaper correspondents accompanied the U.S. troops, and their dispatches, printed all over the country, had most of the public rooting for the Indians all during the period of the retreat.

In return for surrender, Miles and Howard both promised Joseph that he would be returned to his home country in the spring. This promise apparently was made in good faith by the commanders, only to be countered by General William Sherman, who was commander of all the U.S. armies. Despite his professional admiration for the Nez Perce's humane behavior and military strategy, he intended to hang the leaders and send the rest to Indian Territory, never to return to Oregon.

As he was escorting the captives back to Fort Keogh, Miles rode with Joseph and heard his story. He was greatly impressed. He tried to intercede with Sherman on the Nez Perce behalf, reminding the general that the Indians had been promised they could return home in the spring. He was ignored. Later he said angrily, "The Nez Perce trouble was caused by the rascality of their Agent, and the encroachment of the whites."

The captives remained at Keogh for a time before being sent down the river to Fort Lincoln near Bismarck. When they realized that they were not going to be sent back to Oregon, the captives' spirits sank.

In Bismarck there followed another strange event. The Nez Perce, many of whom expected to be hanged, were greeted as heroes, and the whole group was treated to a special dinner. Joseph was guest of honor at a banquet at the Sheridan House, probably the best eating place in town.

The invitation was published in the Bismarck newspaper:

To Joseph, Head Chief of the Nez Perce.

Sir: Desiring to show our kind feelings and the admiration we have for your bravery and humanity, as exhibited in your recent conflict with the forces of the United States, we most cordially invite you to dine with us at the Sheridan House in this city. The dinner to be given at 1½ p.m. today.

If the Nez Perce had not known us so well, they might have thought we were erratic in our inclinations.

Public pressure by supporters of the Nez Perce, including Colonel Miles, led Sherman to change his mind about hanging the leaders, but they were not to be returned to Oregon. Besides Sherman's desire to punish the Indians, political reasons made it impossible to send the Nez Perce home. Murder warrants were out for several of them in Idaho, and Joseph was not considered a hero in Idaho and Montana, where fatalities had occurred before and during the war.

First the Nez Perce were sent to Fort Leavenworth in Kansas, where they were assigned a particularly boggy and unhealthy location. Malaria quickly infected the camp and many people died.

Presently, the survivors were moved to a reservation elsewhere in Kansas, and then to Oklahoma. Meanwhile, Nez Perce who had made it to Canada began filtering back to Idaho. They were not welcome there. Christianized Nez Perce who had stayed behind had no sympathy for the veterans of the war, whom they referred to as "the wild ones." These reservation Indians, along with resident priests, were instrumental in sending the veterans under guard to join Joseph in "the hot place," as the Nez Perce referred to the south.

Joseph grew in moral stature as he pleaded for the welfare of his people. He was visited frequently by various delegations, and was said to "tower over them morally." He journeyed to Washington and spoke to cabinet members, Congressmen, diplomats, and eventually with President Rutherford B. Hayes.

The welfare of the Nez Perce became a national issue. Finally, in 1885, the remaining 268 of them were put on a train for Idaho. There, they were divided into two groups. One group went to the Lapwai Reservation in Idaho, the other to the Colville Reservation in northeastern Washington.

In 1899 Joseph returned to the Wallowa Valley for a visit, and to see if there was any chance of purchasing land there for his people. He was cordially received, according to accounts, but the ranchers who then owned the land would not sell a foot of it for an Indian reserve. That was the end of the old man's hopes of ever returning to live on his ancestral land. He died a few years later.

Thus the story. One of the great privileges of winning a war is that the victors get to write the history. If the government plan to develop the Bears Paw Battlefield is carried out, maybe they could let the Nez Perce themselves tell their own story.

HAVRE

For a while, bumper stickers were floating around proclaiming, "Havre Has It." Some people thought this was a joke, something like "Discover Anaconda."

However, as Hi-Line towns go, Havre truly does have it. It is a sort of capital of all that territory, located somewhere near the middle of it. It has a modern hospital, a mall, a thriving unit of the university system, and many other elements of an up-to-date city on the High Plains. The town is so confident that even an announcement by Burlington Northern that it will lay off about 150 employees did not produce excessive pessimism. "Look at the new Kmart," someone said. "They must know something." Indeed, Havre, already possessed of a Kmart of tolerable size, is getting a new one, reportedly the largest in the state. In 1992, it was being built, out near the junction of Highway 2 and Highway 87 where Canadians can't make the turn without seeing it.

I made an appointment to talk with Lisa Kudrna, representing the Havre Chamber of Commerce. She called in Frank Derosa, retired railroader, businessman, and developer of "Havre Beneath the Streets" to help inform me.

I asked what it was that kept Havre going in the early decades of this century. "Bootlegging," Derosa said. "We were a bootlegging hub."

"Maybe that's why we have such a fine substance abuse center today," Kudrna said, jokingly. And they do have a fine modern building right next to the hospital.

Like the other Hi-Line towns, Havre's history goes back to the railroad's arrival. At first the trains went past the place called Bullhook Bottoms to Fort Assinniboine. Bullhook Bottoms were named after Bullhook Creek, which runs down from what used to be called Bullhook Mountain, but is now called Saddle Butte. Bullhook Mountain got its name from the Indians who had a myth that a buffalo bull used a horn to hook the notch that characterizes the top of the mountain.

The railroad came in 1890, and by 1893 all the local operations had been moved from near Fort Assinniboine to Bullhook Siding. The railroad's repair and maintenance complex at Bullhook, as the community came to be known, was said to be second in size only to St. Paul.

Jim Hill, who owned the railroad and wanted to civilize the country along it, didn't like the name Bullhook, so some pillars of the community met to choose a new name. This group included several Frenchmen, and after turning down the name "France," they decided on "Havre," after Le Havre in France.

Hill felt responsible for the creation of Havre, and wanted it to be couth. In 1899 Hill warned the city fathers that if Havre didn't become more of a model community, he was going to move his railroad works out of town. In 1904, convinced that the town had achieved his high expectations, he arrived there unexpectedly with several financial backers. Upon arrival, Hill and the investors set out on a foot tour. The first interesting event they saw was a patron being literally kicked out of a saloon. Then they saw five men fighting with knives in a vacant lot. And then a man being thrown out a saloon window while another man was leaving by the door, firing a pistol behind him. Town fathers were summoned and given a talking to. According to the legend, the town decided to look clean for Mr. Hill, even if it wasn't. Consequently, they paid train dispatchers east and west to tell them when Hill was coming, so they could sweep things under the rug for the duration of his visit. According to a newspaper account, when Hill came:

"...the gunfighters would be hurried out of town, the key turned in the lock of the worst gambling places, the dance hall girls would put on long dresses and register demureness, the bartenders would shave up and don white vests, and Havre's red blood would, for the nonce, turn to water. With the departure of Hill it would be 'on with the dance, let joy be unconfined,' and the frolic of hell would be resumed."

The town kept a band for the sole purpose of serenading Hill when he came to town.

Regarding the frolic of hell, author Gary A. Wilson in his excellent book, *Honky Tonk Town: Havre's Bootlegging Days,* complained with local pride that Havre does not get due credit for the amount and sheer duration of hell-raising that went on there. Famous rough towns such as Tombstone, Deadwood, and Butte, stayed interesting only for five to 15 years, he wrote, compared to Havre's 50-year frolic.

This was during the reign of Shorty Young, Havre's truly legendary brewer, whoremaster, saloon keeper, bootlegger, and philanthropist.

Young was said to have "materialized out of a boxcar" at Havre in 1894. He seems to have been well-trained at games of chance, and found plenty of employment in Havre. He parlayed his winnings into ownership of a beer hall and hotel, and by 1898 he was proprietor of The Montana European Hotel and Grill, usually known as the Honky Tonk. It had 28 regular employees and two classes of "girls." The five-dollar girls lived nearby in a two-story house, the "Parlour House," and the one-dollar girls worked and lived in little apartments out back, called "cribs." A beer was 20 cents in the Honky Tonk, a dollar on crib row, and three dollars in the Parlour House.

As the 20th century wore on, the bar clientele was changing on the Hi-Line. Cattle was no longer king, cowboys started becoming extinct, and the Army shut down Fort Assinniboine. The new customers were homesteaders. In one day, 250 of them showed up in Havre. In 1913, 1,600 filed homestead claims in Havre in one month. Shorty Young had for sale what these men wanted too, and he got richer and more socially acceptable. He was on the city council, and joined the Eagles, Elks, and Knights of Pythias.

In 1916 Montana elected a reform governor. For a while, Havre held out in its customary fun-loving ways. Law enforcement officers staged fake gambling raids, but the reform forces were not mollified. Then the governor began moving to fire the county attorney. Suddenly all the prostitutes disappeared from Havre. Apparently they had holed up in the hotels, and filled them up. During this disappearance, 3,000 members of the Women's Christian Temperance Union held their state convention in Havre. Nobody seems to know where they stayed. The county attorney eventually was exonerated and business went on.

In the late teens, things toughened up. The drought came on and stayed, and by 1924 Havre was said to have 3,000 people who had nothing to eat but eggs and potatoes.

Then Prohibition came, and the many illegal and profitable evasions of that law came to Havre. Large touring cars began heading to Canada in the afternoon, and returning with heavy loads later at night. Canadian beer was 12 percent alcohol, and came in a unit called a "barrel," which consisted of three burlap bags, each with 24 quart bottles. Price of a barrel in Canada was $20. The same barrel sold in the States for $144. Whiskey was $32 to $50 for a 12-bottle case in Canada, and $35 more in the U.S. When the touring cars returned south, they normally carried 14 barrels of beer and 5 cases of whiskey, with a total value of $2,500.

With this sort of incentive, there soon formed an assembly of international entrepreneurs and importers known informally as "The Havre Bunch." The Havre Bunch was a large-volume operation and reportedly had an arrangement with Mr. Capone of Chicago, to avoid misunderstandings. Booze transported by this group was said to go to every state in the union except Maine. Havre itself was a pretty good customer, with 28 saloons operating. Shorty Young was an executive with The Bunch.

Up until The Bunch was organized, bootlegging had been open to amateurs and independent operators. Afterwards, it no longer was. The Bunch would intercept independent operators and take all or part of their loads.

Besides not being fun anymore, bootlegging got dangerous. In 1920 several men were killed in separate incidents near Simpson, on the border north of Havre.

Things tightened up further when bootlegging was made a felony offense. Government agents patrolled the roads at night, and reportedly had reliable information about when bootleggers left their suppliers in Canada. Much of the action took place west of Havre. Looking at the little prairie villages in that region today—Hingham, Joplin and the rest—it is hard to imagine farmers having their sleep disturbed by the roar of Packards and Cadillacs with machine guns poking out the windows, headed south with a load of hooch for a thirsty and grateful nation. The cars traveled with headlights out, and when the roads were snowed in during the winter they sometimes took shortcuts across farmers' fields.

All good things must come to an end, and in 1932 the second Roosevelt got elected and promptly ended Prohibition. Two rail cars of 3.2 beer arrived in Havre on April 10, 1933, to the general satisfaction of the drinking public.

Shorty Young stayed in business, but fell upon hard times. He died in bed in the Parlour House in 1944. Upon Shorty's death, the crowd of faithful that had occupied his last bar moved down the street to another. Within a few years, even these die-hards had died, and the memory of Havre's wooly days began to recede.

Shorty wrote out his own will, and divided his worldly goods among three groups: the Elks, the Eagles, and the Masonic Lodge. He belonged to the first two of these, but was blackballed by the Masons for being a lowlife. He specified that the money was for "the education, care, and maintenance of the needy of Havre."

BIG BUD: THEY DON'T MAKE 'EM LIKE THAT ANYMORE

Anybody who has paid attention to farming for the last 20 or 30 years has seen the farm tractor grow from Old MacDonald's familiar little unit with the two big wheels and two little wheels into massive jobs with four sets of duals and all wheels driving and the farmer listening to rap tunes in an air-conditioned cab.

Various forces led to this change. "There are fewer farms now, and the farmers that are left are consolidating their horsepower," according to Ron Harmon, who still carries the title of CEO of the Big Bud company in Havre, though the firm is now part of another business. "Consolidating horsepower" means that a farmer might trade two medium-sized tractors that used to go with two farms for one larger tractor on his merged acreage.

In 1969 two Havre men, Bud Nelson and Willie Hensley, decided to start building really big tractors here. Harmon explained the concept developed by Nelson and Hensley.

Partly, he said, the Big Bud idea was to take technology already used for other purposes and adapt it to farm tractors. Nelson and Hensley looked to the mining and construction industries, where heavy-duty

84

equipment had been developed. Developing and testing such technology can cost millions of dollars, Harmon said, but after it has been developed and perfected, it becomes standard equipment and the components can be purchased anywhere. Big Bud took what it needed for its mighty machines.

Besides using thoroughly tested technology, the Big Bud tractor incorporated easy serviceability. The cab and hood could be hydraulically lifted out of the way to allow access to the engine and drive train. Along with accessibility, the tractor was built with a skid system that allowed easy removal of engine, transmission, and other major components. If a tractor needed a different gear ratio than it had, the transmission could be readily replaced, for example. Harmon said that the result of these innovations was a more universal, easier-to-service tractor than those offered by the competition.

Easy service was the frosting on the cake, but Big Bud's main selling point was horsepower. The smallest Bud ever built was 250 horsepower, the largest was 980. Only one 980-horse unit was built. It had eight 8-foot-tall tires, a V-16 Detroit twin turbo diesel, and weighed 130,000 pounds. This biggest of Buds was initially operated in California by Rossi Brothers, who used it to replace a D-9 Caterpillar. Big Bud was used to pull king-size farm equipment, including a 15-shank sub-soiler that worked 40 inches deep, and a 60-foot plow that plowed 12 inches deep. The D-9 farmed 15 acres a day. Big Bud farmed 15 acres an hour. Most of the Big Bud tractors were in the 500 to 600 horsepower category. For comparison, the largest tractors made by the major manufacturers in 1992 were 375 horsepower.

Production of Big Bud started slowly. By 1974 the company was manufacturing 10 tractors a year. By 1979 it had nearly 200 employees and was making 100 tractors a year. A total of about 700 tractors were built, of which 350 were sold through the Havre dealership. Some Big Buds made long trips to their jobs. Because of their standardized components, the tractors could be readily serviced and repaired worldwide. "Australia, the Philippines, the Middle East; you can go into a store and buy parts that will fit a Big Bud," Harmon said. Dole and Del Monte purchased several for their pineapple farms in Hawaii, for example.

Big Bud plowed into trouble in 1979. The company that supplied transmissions for the big machines had problems of its own, and for nine months there were no transmissions for Big Bud. This led to financial difficulty that culminated with the Big Bud company going into bankruptcy in 1982. The company then changed hands, being purchased by Meissner Brothers of Chester, Montana (now of Havre).

Meissner has built a few Big Buds since 1985, Harmon said, but it is primarily a retail brand company. Meissner is the regional center for big equipment, Harmon said. "We specialize in the big stuff for the 'broad acre farms' in the Golden Triangle and southern Canada. It's still who we are." He said the sale and repair of used Big Buds is still a major portion of Meissner's business.

At the moment, Harmon said, there is a much larger need for tractor rebuilding than for new tractors. Farmers find it more economical to run their old tractors as long as they can and then rebuild them than to buy new ones. "In 1980," Harmon said, "farmers would trade in their tractors when they had 2,000 hours on their engines. Now I see them coming in for trade with 5,000 or 10,000 hours." For comparison, if one were to drive an automobile for 100,000 miles at an average speed of 50 miles per hour, the engine would run 2,000 hours.

Harmon said that there has been a terrific shakeout in the tractor industry in the last 15 years or so up to 1992, particularly in the 4-wheel-drive segment. The 4-wheelers came most strongly into the market in 1980, when 10,000 were sold nationwide. Sales then slowed down until they bottomed out at 1,800 nationwide in 1986. "Annual sales nationwide now are about 4,000 4-wheel-drive tractors a year," Harmon said. "We're never going to see sales like 1980 again."

Decreasing sales in the 1980s led to major shifts in the tractor manufacturing industry, with most companies either consolidating with other companies or going out of business. In tractors over 400 horsepower, only Big Bud is left. Steiger, which formerly made tractors as big as 525 horsepower, has been purchased by Case/International Harvester, and no longer produces a machine over 375 horses. None of these agglomerated tractor companies is interested in making a tractor of over 400 horsepower for the few hundred buyers that would be interested, Harmon said.

"The bottom line is that there is still a market out there for big tractors. For us, it's a heck of a chance," Harmon said. He said that Meissner Brothers still own all the tooling and equipment needed to make Big Bud. It is conceivable that one of these days the big ones will start rolling out again.

The 1992 price of new Big Bud is as follows, according to Harmon:
700 hp, $300,000
500 hp, $225,000
400 hp, $159,000

And the prices of used machines are as follows:
400 hp, $40,000 to $60,000
500 hp, $50,000 to $80,000
600 hp, $100,000 to $150,000

HAVRE BENEATH THE STREETS

I asked Frank Derosa, "What about these tunnels?"

"Don't call them tunnels," he said. "People don't like tunnels. Just call it 'Havre Beneath the Streets'."

Okay. Frank Derosa is a retired railroad man and semi-retired Havre businessman who has taken on the task of developing a tourist attraction from a mostly abandoned underground portion of Havre. The history of this underground portion of the town is a bit hazy. "We think it might have started after the fire," he said. The fire, in 1904, pretty much wiped Havre out, and some businessmen apparently reopened their businesses in their basements until the town could rebuild.

And of course there were the Chinese. Many Chinese came with the building of the railroad across northern Montana, and a lot of them remained afterwards. There was strong prejudice against them and they disappeared from the streets after dark, Derosa said. Nobody knew where they went, but the theory is that they had safe houses in the underground. One part of the Havre Beneath the Streets tour will include a large room that Derosa thinks was used as a safe house and probably as a bordello at another time. Numbers are painted on the wall of this room every 10 feet or so, and apparently there was a bed under each number.

Derosa said the Havre Beneath the Streets project is partly to commemorate the little-known subterranean history of Havre, and partly to provide a tourist attraction. Getting information about the history has been difficult. "Old-timers don't want to talk about it," Derosa said. At one time, Derosa said, large passageways ran under the sidewalks of downtown Havre. In some places passages apparently crossed beneath the streets from side to side.

In his book, *Honky Tonk Town,* Gary A. Wilson said that steam tunnels ran throughout the town, and people could walk upright from building to building without being seen above ground. Wilson said that Shorty Young had his own set of tunnels connecting only his buildings.

When Highway 2 was upgraded through town, the space under the sidewalks was filled in. The cross-street connecting tunnels may still be there; nobody seems to know. The old openings from the basements are sealed off. Havre Beneath the Streets includes the spaces under two sidewalks that ran perpendicular to Highway 2 and were not filled in. In places the sidewalks are studded with squares of glass, badly cracked and chipped and purple with age. These glass squares allow an amazing amount of light into the large space, not a tunnel, under the sidewalks. Underground businesses had windows opening into this space.

Derosa said that when Havre Beneath the Streets is complete, it will include reconstructions of a dozen or so businesses of the sort that were there originally, furnished with the original equipment as much as possible.

The opium den to be included in the displays will be in the space that Derosa believes such a den had occupied originally. More than one such den was known to exist in Havre in its boom years. Another display will be devoted to Shorty Young's office.

Bill Roper, a Cut Bank resident who was born and raised in Havre, had a personal demonstration that at least one of Shorty Young's establishments made good use of a tunnel. When Roper was a young man he went to Northern Montana College, and being young, he wanted to do what young people like to do. Dancing mainly, and one of Shorty Young's places was the best dancing spot in town. "There were girls and booze there too," he said, "but all I wanted was to dance." The problem was that the college was safeguarding the morals of its students by putting Shorty Young's businesses off limits. A student caught there could be thrown out of school.

Being a man of sound morals, Bill went to Shorty's place anyway. Usually there wasn't any problem, but one time a road crew was working nearby and a lot of guys on the crew were from Butte. Bill was dancing up a storm when these Buttes came in and started a big scrap. "They were breaking the mirrors and busting the furniture," Bill said, and there was no way to get out. This was serious because the cops were sure to come and drag Bill down to the station despite his sound morals. When the college found out, his days as a student might be limited.

The black men who made up the band saw Bill's dilemma, and they were not in the mood for any trips to the police station either. They had the solution. They motioned for Bill to follow, and they disappeared under the stage. After 100 feet or so of tunnel, Bill found himself kicking cinders around in the Great Northern railyard, well away from the disorder at Shorty's place.

As of 1992, Havre Beneath the Streets had a ways to go before it was going to be ready for tourists. "When it's ready depends on how much help I get," Derosa said. He has only one regular helper, and he pointed out that he is not a young man. He was busy installing some reclaimed hardwood flooring, a time-consuming and strenuous task. "Don't tell people a time it's going to be ready," he said. Some publicity jumped the gun and said the tour would begin during the 1992 season, and calls immediately started coming in. "A lot of people are interested in this sort of thing," Derosa said.

NORTHERN MONTANA COLLEGE

One of the anchors to life on the Hi-Line is Northern Montana College in Havre. With an enrollment of 1,586 students (1991-1992), the school provides vital educational services to Hi-Line residents. Lynn Hamilton, Information Officer at the college, pointed out that 96 percent of all the teachers and nurses graduated from Northern remain in Montana.

Hamilton said the fastest-growing program at Northern is nurse training. The nursing program at Northern is different from most in that it offers a two-year associate degree. After nursing students have earned the associate degree, they can take the test to become certified registered nurses. Upon certification, they are qualified to continue their studies to obtain the four-year baccalaureate degree. The baccalaureate degree opens many career doors to the nurses, Hamilton said.

The presence of Northern in Havre makes it possible for nurses to work part-time and go to school part-time to upgrade their skills. This has benefits all around. "Health care in rural areas is a real hot issue right now," Hamilton said.

Teaching and nursing are two of Northern's five focus areas. The others are liberal arts and sciences, business, and technologies such as computer science and agricultural mechanics. Students can earn a degree in business, with a minor in a technical area. "A lot of our business majors select a minor in some aspect of farming, such as agricultural mechanics," Hamilton said, adding that graduates in technology commonly go to work at the entry level for a company such as GM or Toyota and rise quickly up the ranks.

Besides its customary role of preparing young people for life in a technological society, there are indications that Northern also is helping to retrain "displaced workers" who have lost or given up on their old jobs and are training for new ones. "In 1980," Hamilton said, "eighty percent of our enrollment was traditional students, those just out of high school. Now, the average age of students at Northern is thirty-six."

Most of the students at Northern are from the Hi-Line. A fair number of them are needed at home to work on the farm during spring and fall quarters, which results in Northern having its highest enrollment during winter quarter. Starting in the fall of 1992, the school went to the semester system, and it was necessary to make some accommodations for the students who had farm work to do. "We split some courses, ag mechanics for example, into two sections so students could take one now and one later."

As with other publicly funded colleges and universities in Montana, tight funds have made the future uncertain. However, as Hamilton pointed out, Northern Montana College provides many important services that benefit Montana, and any reduction of such services would be keenly felt, especially on the Hi-Line.

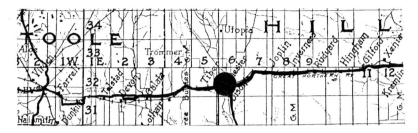

CHESTER

Running west from Havre, the land shows what is left of Jim Hill's dream. Almost unfailingly, a little town straddles the rails every six miles, with grain elevators and water tanks breaking the flatness of the plains. Kremlin, Gildford, Hingham, Rudyard, Inverness, Joplin. Then the traveler arrives at Chester, "Heart of the Hi-Line," as it takes pleasure in calling itself.

Chester is no metropolis, but it does provide a sort of anchor for the smaller towns in the vicinity. It has medical facilities, including a hospital and nursing home, and its newspaper, the *Liberty County Times,* covers sports and other events for the towns as far east as Kremlin. The town even boasts a manufacturing plant. The Wiese Corporation in 1991 reopened an idle factory that makes cultivator shovels, and the plant now cranks out about 2,000 of the shovels per day.

Chester was named by a Great Northern telegraph operator in honor of his boyhood home of Chester, Pennsylvania. The town was incorporated in 1910. In 1919 Chester defeated Joplin in an election to determine which town would be the county seat of the newly created Liberty County.

Jopliners had another inning, however, and they boosted petitions to get the boundaries of the county drawn the way they wanted them. In order to keep track of this treacherous activity, the Chester interests stationed a man on the water tower in Inverness to keep them informed where the cars from Joplin went with their petition. Then the Chesterites lobbied the same citizens visited by the Jopliners, and won that election too.

Just to the north of town are the Sweetgrass Hills, volcanic remnants that stand well above the surrounding plain and provide landmarks for viewers over thousands of square miles. Local pride regarding these mountains runs high, and recent mining proposals have met a lack of enthusiasm that is rare in any area where new economic development is eagerly sought.

Basically, Chester is a sleepy farming town, and most of the people there seem to like it that way. The Lions Club installed a pleasantly rustic rest stop on the east edge of town to provide relief for travelers and possibly slow them down enough to spend a dollar or two, but the Hi-Line from Havre to Shelby is free of tourist inducements. There's not even a stop sign to impede their hell-for-leather roaring to Glacier Park, and then back again. Amtrak doesn't stop there, and passengers on the train probably don't notice anything between Shelby and Havre. If any of the folks in Chester want life in the fast lane, they know where the fast lane is. It's not in Chester. If some former residents find life in the fast lane a little too hectic, Chester will be there for them.

RICHARD BUKER, JR., M.D.

Ask anybody in Chester what makes their community different from others and most of them will say the name of one man: Dr. Richard Buker, Jr. Dr. Buker has been nationally recognized as a sort of phenomenon. Earlier in 1992, for example, he was honored by a national organization as Rural Health Practitioner of the Year. "It wasn't deserved," he told me when I interviewed him. "They didn't look at all the rural health practitioners that might have deserved it." The firmness of his manner made it easy for me to imagine him saying, "Those tonsils have got to come out," or "Give up those cigarettes or die."

An award he is much prouder of is the Silver Spur Award for community service, given him by a Shelby radio station. He seemed gratified that it came from people who knew of his work first-hand. For a contrary view, he said, "you could talk to some of my less ardent admirers."

Dr. Buker was born in Boston of parents who were medical missionaries. As a boy he lived in Burma and India, and went to prep school in New York State. Except for one brief stint, he never attended a public school, which made it interesting when he was elected to the school board in Chester.

After Yale Medical School, he went into the military. "I felt an obligation," he said, noting that he held a student deferment from service during World War II. In 1954, after an assignment in the Philippines, Dr. Buker was returned to the U.S. where the military assigned him to a retirement board. His task would have been to review the condition of retirees and recommend what pension they should get. "I went to medical school to make sick people well," Buker said. "I had always wanted to do rural medical practice." Buker sent enquiries to states without medical schools, asking whether they needed any rural physicians. He received numerous responses.

He then took leave and traveled around to look at the prospects. In a little North Dakota town where he went to interview, the townspeople directed him to a fleabag hotel where he had to spend the weekend, and to top that off the only eating place in town was closed until Monday. He went without food from Friday to Monday. "I was one hungry guy," he said. His next stop was Chester. In Chester they not only insisted on feeding him and putting him up but they drove him around to show him the outstanding features of the country.

They were pretty high on the prospects of Tiber Dam, and they pointed out thousands of acres that were going to be irrigated. None of it happened. "It's a great no-purpose dam," he said.

Dr. Buker was not impressed with the physical qualities of Chester when he first saw it in 1954. "There were no trees or grass. They had this soda water that you couldn't grow anything with. It was a grimy little prairie town."

In a later conversation with Dr. Buker's wife, Jean, she recalled the day she came home to Chester for the first time. "Where are we?" she asked, somewhat bewildered. "This is home," Dr. Buker said. "Why are we here?" she asked. She recalled the doctor's explanation—"Of all the places I visited, this was the one that I thought was least likely to succeed in getting a doctor."

The people, on the other hand, Dr. Buker found to be quite remarkable, a judgment that has grown stronger over the years. "Chester was the only place I looked at where nobody had a vested interest in getting a doctor. Other places, there was always somebody who had a vacant office he wanted to rent, or a pharmacist who wasn't getting any business because there was no doctor."

Buker told the community leaders he would need a house for himself and his family. They bought him a five-bedroom house, and were going to let him live in it free. He insisted on paying rent, and thinks it might have been $100 a month. He volunteered to provide his services free to the indigent in the county, as a supplement to the puny rent.

Before he could actually begin his medical practice in Chester, Dr. Buker had to go back to California and get his family. That should have been easy enough, but wasn't. Coming across the California desert at night, the car caught fire. A mechanic had set the brakes too tight. "Funny what you think of at a time like that," Dr. Buker said. Contemplating his flaming car, he made his selection quickly: "I got out the kids, my military orders, and my fishing pole."

The family silver, a wedding present, didn't get rescued. The family decided that Mrs. Buker and the kids would go back temporarily to Mrs. Buker's family home in Boston while the doctor came to Chester and got settled. After his family left, Dr. Buker went back to the desert, took one last look at the family silver melted in the sand, and caught the bus for Chester. "He came like a peddler with a suitcase," Mrs. Buker said. "It will be 38 years ago tomorrow that I got here on the bus," he said when I talked to him on July 30, 1992. "I've been struggling along in this job ever since. Now the bus doesn't even come to Chester anymore."

There had been a doctor in town, but he had been broken by stress and overwork. Jean Buker said her husband dedicated himself to carrying on the work that had been started by his predecessor.

"The hospital was closed when I got here. The county had $1,400 to open the hospital with, and we soon got it up and running. I had one registered nurse and one licensed practical nurse. One of us per shift." The hospital had ten rooms.

"Today, we have a two-and-a-half-million-dollar plant here, with eighty jobs depending on it. We have fifteen nurses, lab technicians, x-ray technicians...it's quite a change. For the first fifteen years I was here I did all the x-ray and lab work myself. I had never taken an x-ray before I got here. I had to run EKGs. I had never run one of them before.

"I think we provide reasonably good rural health care. One of the reasons it's good to have health care in local communities is that people will come in sooner when they don't have to travel so far. That way, we can catch serious problems like cancer and infections before they get too far advanced. One of these days when I get time I'm going to write a paper about the effects of rural health care on mortality."

Dr. Buker has more time than he once did. "For the first five years I was here I saw at least one patient every day." For nine and a half of the 38 years that Dr. Buker has been at Chester, he has been the only doctor in town. Other doctors have come and gone. One was Buker's brother, who stayed fifteen years and then moved to Whitefish. "Whitefish needs doctors like a hole in the head. There's one on every street corner," he said. In contrast, the hospital in Chester has files on over 5,000 patients, in a county with just over 2,000 residents.

Dr. Buker has occasionally had medical students come to work with him, with the idea that they might eventually return. "They always say, as they leave, 'Gee, it was a great experience, but I just couldn't do this'," he said. These students have been pretty consistent about going on to the faculties of eminent medical schools, he said.

Once the retired dean of Yale Medical School came to visit Buker and watch him work. "Here was a man who spent most of his professional life educating medical students. He said to me, 'I notice that most patients are either very old or very young. I didn't know that.'" The visiting professor also thought Buker's fees were too low. "He heard me counseling people about their emotional problems, and he said, 'That's worth sixty dollars an hour.' I was charging five dollars for an office call at the time."

Medical schools today don't do a very good job of teaching students what they need to know for a rural practice, Buker said. He said a lot of internists seem to be trained mostly to determine which specialist patients should be directed to. "Medical school graduates today are weak in a lot of areas—the sciences, physiology, pharmacology, radiology, for example. To do rural medicine you need trauma training, and some surgical skills. Students in training for family practice get no surgery training. The average kid out of medical school has no idea how to treat a cold, a sore back, or a sprained ankle. That's most of what we do here."

Dr. Buker has done what he can to encourage students from the Hi-Line to become doctors and come to Chester to practice. He helps oversee a scholarship fund to pay the costs of attending medical school. Several students have been funded, five from Liberty County. Only one of the doctors trained has returned to the Hi-Line, and practices in Havre. "They'd rather go to Whitefish," Buker said.

So what's going to happen to the Chester hospital when Dr. Buker isn't there anymore? "I don't think anyone is indispensable, but they tell me that when I leave, it will fall, and eighty jobs depend on me," he said. Another doctor practices in Chester, but Dr. Buker said he is sure the other doctor would not be willing to carry the whole burden himself, should Buker retire. "I'm sixty-eight now and I'd like to do a little less. I notice myself forgetting things more. I watched my father practice after he got too old, and I want to avoid that." Buker's father and mother are both residents in the nursing home addition of the hospital.

The nursing home is a source of pride with Buker. He said his interest in nursing homes goes back to when he was a student. "I worked for an undertaker when I was in medical school. I got five dollars for every body I moved. I used to go with the undertaker to nursing homes to get bodies. In those days, nursing homes were not regulated, and some of the conditions were just horrendous. I told myself that if I was ever in a position to do something about that, I would."

After he had been in Chester a while, Buker saw the need for a nursing home. "I had an old guy that needed a nursing home, and I had to send him to Jordan. Then I had another old guy and I had to send him to Harlowton." So Buker got busy and helped the community build the facility. "We built a wing and it filled up, and we built another wing and it filled up. Now we have forty-seven beds and we're not quite full yet."

Buker said he visits every resident in the nursing home every day. Nursing home inspectors come around and ask how often he visits the residents, and when he tells them "every day," they think he's lying, he said.

Buker takes rueful note of the encroachment of government into medical practice. He pointed out that the entire space that was the hospital when he came to Chester is now taken up with administrative people, mostly to fulfill government requirements.

"Our x-rays are supposed to be looked at by radiologists. We don't have a radiologist, and we have to rely on a rent-a-radiologist service. So we find ourselves in the middle of the night with a sick kid, and where is the radiologist? I've kept track of my record in reading x-rays, and I find I miss something about three times out of a hundred."

Buker also does autopsies. "The state medical examiner comes around and says, 'You're not a certified pathologist,' and I say, 'That's true, but who else do you see here to do it?'"

Dr. Buker has advice for rural communities trying to recruit a doctor. "Don't offer them a lot of money. There are doctors who go from community to community to take advantage of financial incentives. Then when the incentive is gone, they're off to the next place. There's a fair amount of money to be made in rural practice, but the main incentive has to be personal and professional satisfaction."

Not everything that happens to a rural doctor is satisfying. "I've been sued a few times, but I've never been found guilty. It's always somebody from outside the county who sues. If you don't get sued, you aren't doing anything. I believe that it's better to act than to do nothing. Medical practice is not an exact science. Sometimes you don't know what you're looking at for sure. I treat probabilities."

95

Obstetrics is a substantial portion of Dr. Buker's practice, and he has welcomed many of the present residents of the Hi-Line into the world. How many births has he attended? He doesn't know exactly, he said, but probably over 2,000. More than 200 of those were during his military duty before he came to Chester, and many more were in Pakistan, where he spent a year as a medical volunteer. But he's done plenty on the Hi-Line too. "I'm starting into the third generation," he said, having delivered the grandchildren of other babies he delivered. "Not too many so far, but we have many second generation births," he said. This points up Dr. Buker's contention that continuity of care is an important aspect of rural practice. It also is one of the things that is missing from most other medical practice, he said. "Sub-specialists tend to look just at a system rather than at a whole person. And there is another thing that disturbs me. Doctors will look at a patient and say, 'That's not my field, go see somebody else.' Neurosurgeons are the worst for this. A lot of patient neglect and abuse results from this attitude. Many patients are over-awed about going to a doctor anyway, and when they get sent away like that, they may give up on treatment."

Another busy aspect of Dr. Buker's practice is trauma, which is the treatment of injuries. On the average, he sews up two cuts and sets one broken bone each day, he said. Trauma also provides some of the most hair-raising cases. Dr. Buker remembers one young man who was "the sickest person I ever treated who lived through it." As a result of an auto accident, this young man had 13 broken ribs, fractures of both arms and both legs, and a ruptured spleen. "I stuck with him for days. He's still alive, and he has 13 kids."

Besides bringing people into the world, Dr. Buker eventually sees many of them out. "One of the impressive things about people up here is that they know how to face death," he said. "They are a great inspiration to me." He told of one 90-year-old man whom he diagnosed with a terminal disease. "I told him the situation, and that we could keep him going for a while with transfusions. He had some business that needed to be taken care of, so he took some transfusions. Then he came in one day and said he didn't need any more transfusions. He died with dignity and equanimity. Another man refused transfusions from the time his illness was diagnosed, and soon died. "He was alert up to within thirty minutes of his death," Dr. Buker said. "They're a bunch of old survivors up here. They have great attitudes and values. And they have some good investment ideas too."

I asked Dr. Buker what he does for fun. "I work," he said. "Oh, I can't say I never have any time off. I had a week last spring. But mostly it doesn't do any good for me to try to get away. They just hunt me down wherever I am." He does have some free time, though, and he likes to hunt and fish, read history, and work at photography.

Besides being the doctor, Buker is active in many community affairs. He was on the school board for many years, for example. "When I ran for school board, people would say, 'Well, what are you going to do?' and I would say, 'Well, I'm not going to save you any money.' There was a lot that I thought the schools needed, and it cost money. We did a survey of the county and they said they wanted the high school to emphasize college prep. The school didn't have any foreign language, and it was weak in science and English. We had some battles, and eventually we got foreign language and beefed up the sciences. We weren't so lucky improving the English program. I guess I lost more battles than I won." He mentioned that he was the only college graduate on the school board when he was first elected, and that three of the five members had not completed high school. He eventually had to leave the school board to deal with the mountains of paperwork that the government came to require of medical practitioners.

Dr. Buker offered me a tour of the hospital and nursing home. As he showed me the x-ray room he pointed at the big machine at the heart of it and said, "That thing cost three hundred thousand dollars. They won't let me touch it. That's the first sure sign they think I'm getting senile."

In the laboratory, he said, "I'll tell you a story about this laboratory. An old farmer came up to me one day and said, 'What do you need for this hospital?' I said, 'A laboratory.' So the old guy wrote a check for fifty thousand dollars and said, 'Here, build a laboratory.'

"And then a bit later, another old guy said he needed to do something about his taxes, and he wrote me another fifty thousand dollar check. And we said, 'Gee, we need a hospital to go with this lab,' so the community raised four hundred and thirty thousand dollars for a new wing, and it was all paid for in advance, no public money."

After my tour, Dr. Buker gave me a ride to my vehicle. His vehicle reminded me of the saying that third-class riding beats first-class walking. It is an old Ford pickup that seems to have been the loser in one or more demolition derbies. "Comes from teaching teenagers to drive," he said. "I can't get insurance on it any more. But the motor runs fine, and the brakes are good. If it starts and stops, what more do you need?" Life on the Hi-Line brings a practical frame of mind.

HEAVY INDUSTRY IN CHESTER

The Wiese Corporation, based in Perry, Iowa, began operating in Chester on November 16, 1991. In its first manufacturing season, running through spring of 1992, the plant made about 125,000 cultivator shovels. The company intends eventually to sell shovels throughout Montana, but the demand has been so high that the shovels either haven't made it to some stores or have been immediately sold out.

Plant manager Curt Plumb said Wiese located in Chester partly because the plant was already there, having formerly been occupied by Liberty Manufacturing, a shovel-making operation that failed in business, and partly because the company wanted to make shovels in the wheat country. The Chester plant is Wiese's only plant that manufactures these particular shovels. Until Wiese started operating in Chester, it sold shovels made in Brazil. The Chester plant thus not only provides jobs in Chester, but brings a part of American industry home, Plumb said.

Despite the intention of selling as many shovels locally as possible, Plumb said the first sale the plant made was to Saudi Arabia. "I didn't even know they farmed over there," he said. He noted that the Saudis must have liked the product because they ordered a second batch. Other orders went to Canada and Australia.

Plumb said one advantage of the plant being located in Montana is that the users of the shovels can provide feedback to the makers. He said the shovels from the Chester plant have been modified in line with recommendations by Montana farmers.

Steel for the shovels is American-made and trucked from Alton, Illinois. Truckers have a tough time finding loads for the return trip, Plumb said.

The plant employs nine people, including Plumb. The operation runs 10-hour shifts, and makes about 2,000 pieces per day, Plumb said. In the fall, winter and spring, the plant runs five 10-hour shifts to increase production. During the summer, work weeks are four 10-hour days.

Plumb, who is from Iowa, said he likes working in a small town. "Everybody here bends over backwards for us," he said. "If we need to borrow some heavy equipment, for example, all we do is let people know and it will be here."

Steel comes into the plant in quarter-inch-thick flat plate. A sheer press cuts the steel into triangles of the right size, either 14⅞ or 11½ inches, depending on what size shovels are being made. The triangles then go into a natural-gas-fired furnace that heats the steel to 1800° F. The interior of the furnace rotates the steel slowly around to the other side, where a workman reaches in with a long pair of tongs and extracts the hot triangles, one at a time. He places each triangle into the plater press, which bevels the edge.

When this operation is complete, in a matter of seconds, another workman with tongs grabs the piece and moves it to the punch/trim press alongside the plater press. In a single operation, this press cuts notches in the steel, trims the wings that are formed in the process, and punches and countersinks bolt holes. The forming press then gives the piece its final shape, after which the hot steel is placed in the oil-quench tank for hardening. Plumb said it takes about 20 seconds for the steel to make the trip from the furnace to the quench tank. This requires fast work by the "hot steel" men. Plumb noted that orders have been increasing, but said that Wiese has no immediate plans to expand production facilities beyond what they are at Chester.

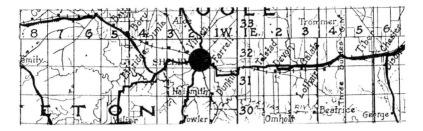

SHELBY

The town of Shelby was named after Peter Shelby, an employee of the Great Northern Railway. He seems to have been something of an ingrate, and is in the record for his remark: "I don't know what Manvel was thinking of when he named that mudhole God-forsaken place after me. It will never amount to a damn."

It is true that up to that time, about 1890, the prospects for Shelby may have been dim. One observer noted that the site of Shelby "was a flat cheerless location skirted by hills upon the south...." One might note that the Hi-Line had many cheerless locations that became towns.

One thing the Shelby site had was the 19th-century whisky trade along the Whoop-Up Trail between Fort Benton and the booze retail establishments in Canada, including Fort Whoop-Up, Fort Slide-Out, Fort Stand-Off, and others. On a hill by the highway just a mile or two east of Shelby is a historical monument to the Whoop-Up Trail, which passed that place. A few miles farther east near Galata is the Bootlegger Trail, which stood brisk traffic earlier this century when the tide of illegal whiskey reversed.

The Great Northern made it to Shelby in 1890. The Great Falls and Canada narrow-gauge railroad had opened for business between Lethbridge and Great Falls in 1890, and it also went through Shelby, which was known for a time as "Shelby Junction." Presently, the two railroads were paralleled by two roads, which eventually became Highway 2 and Interstate 15.

Ranching and homesteading played big in the early history of Shelby. In 1922 oil was discovered north of town, and continues to figure in the local economy, though at a greatly reduced scale. The euphoria and boosterism that followed the oil discovery led the little town, still sunk in the mud and dust in 1923, to play host to the immortal heavyweight title fight between Jack Dempsey and Tommy Gibbons on July 4, 1923. The fight made Shelby famous for a season, and the fame has not completely died.

John F. Kavanagh, publisher of the Shelby *Promoter,* told me that the second-hand memory of the great fight is still green with many a sports fan. "They come to Shelby because of the history," he said. Nearly 70 years after the fight, the young boxer from Great Falls, Todd Foster, fought in Shelby, and the nostalgia was thick, although few witnesses to the 1923 fight still survive. There is something magical still about the words, "fight in Shelby."

Today, Shelby is a little Hi-Line town with the problems of Hi-Line towns. However, it has advantages that other towns lack. The two railroads and highways are important contributors to the local economy. "We looked at those trains and trucks going by for years and tried to think of some way to get them to stop," Kavanagh said.

Today, many of them stop. One major reason is the Northern Express Transportation Authority (NETA), a joint creation of Shelby and Toole County. So far, NETA's major accomplishment has been the construction of a "bulk transload facility," which makes it possible to load dry commodities such as fertilizer from trucks to trains or trains to trucks. The facility has four silos where commodities can be stored, or they can be transferred directly, which is what is usually done.

Mark Cole, who runs the facility, said it has been handling between 1,500 and 3,000 tons per month. He said the facility provides many advantages in time and money for shippers and consumers. For example, if Canada wants to ship a load of fertilizer to Idaho, it can be moved out of Canada by truck much more quickly than by train. Once in Shelby, however, it can be shipped to Idaho much more economically by train.

Even a casual observer can see that things are happening in Shelby. Just outside of town near the crossroads, for example, a large PAMIDA store offers relief to Canadians who are in a hurry to spend money. Kavanagh said the PAMIDA store has been good for Shelby in various ways. "It forced the downtown stores to stay open longer, and it increased customer traffic and improved business. They come down here headed for Great Falls. We get 'em on the way down and on the way back up," he said. Stores in Shelby send 10,000 shopping fliers through the mail to residents of southern Canada, and this helps too, Kavanagh said.

Kavanagh said Shelby is doing better in part because the town, its mayor, Larry Bonderud, and the City Council have taken an aggressive approach to solving problems. Part of the reason the PAMIDA store came to Shelby, Kavanagh said, is that Shelby offered to extend water and sewer services to the store, although it is outside the city. "The mayor went out and got grant money for the services," he said.

Another symptom of optimism in Shelby is the successful recruitment of four new physicians. "We got two general practitioners, a radiologist and a surgeon," Kavanagh said, crediting the hospital board for making the effort to get the doctors.

Along with the new doctors has come a mini-housing boom. "Several new houses are being built," Kavanagh said. "There was a long dry spell without a nail pounded here. Now there's even a spec house [house built by someone who thinks he can sell it]. I think they are going to try to sell a house to one of the doctors. Doctors don't want to live in your ordinary thirty- or forty- or fifty-thousand-dollar house."

Shelby maintains the rivalry with Cut Bank that has existed ever since the railroad came through. One of the new doctors was lured away from Cut Bank. Shelby's hospital, which is now starting to pull out of the red, is drawing patients from Cut Bank. MacDonald's considered locating at Shelby but decided to go to Cut Bank instead. Hardee's considered moving in but didn't, and the Town Pump company is intending to build a Town House Motel with meeting rooms.

"I'm proud of the people of Shelby for trying to make Shelby more than an agricultural community," Kavanagh said. "A few years ago, things were lousy around here. Crops weren't worth a damn, and things looked bad. Now, there's optimism in the community."

FAMOUS FISTICUFFS IN SHELBY

Montana trivia: How many banks went broke after the famous heavyweight championship bout between Jack Dempsey and Tommy Gibbons in Shelby?

While we're thinking about that, let's go back to the events that led up to that famous day and year, July 4, 1923. The number of words written about those events probably totals a few million. Those of us who have waited until now to inform ourselves are lucky to have in hand a recent book by a man who claims the whole thing was his idea, James W. "Body" Johnson. Johnson, who died in 1991, was a principal in the action from the beginning, and he wrote with the rare advantage of being the last living witness. Body Johnson was a son of Shelby mayor and banker James A. Johnson, who was left holding the largest empty bag after the fight.

The younger Johnson wrote in his book, *The Fight that Won't Stay Dead,* that the idea of offering to hold the fight in Shelby came to him out of the blue one day when he saw a news story about someone in Montreal having offered Jack Dempsey, the heavyweight champion, $100,000 to fight in the Canadian city.

It wasn't boxing that was on Johnson's mind, it was publicity. Oil had recently been struck near Shelby and the place was booming, real-estate prices were skyrocketing, but Shelby, though it had 575 citizens, was unjustly unknown to the outside world. This was discouraging to Johnson, who was in the real-estate business. If more people knew about Shelby, he figured, they would flock there to get in on the ground floor of prosperity. In no time Shelby would be "the Tulsa of the West," as it sometimes advertised itself. These possibilities flashed before Johnson's eyes when he saw a burg as undistinguished as Montreal garnering free newspaper ink for the mere act of having sent one telegram to Jack Kearns, Dempsey's manager.

When it came to sending telegrams, Johnson could do it as well as anybody. With the newspaper still in his hand, he said, "Let's wire Jack Kearns and offer him $200,000." A local boxing authority said Tommy Gibbons was the likely opponent, though most people had never heard of him. The telegram went out and sure enough, Kearns wired back and said he was interested. This was the beginning of a torrent of free publicity for the Tulsa of the West. Johnson was in Helena when he heard about Kearns' response, so he took the trouble of going to the governor and the attorney general and asking their blessing for the fight. They of course agreed, and this provided more publicity.

Riding high, Johnson did not return directly to Shelby, but meandered through Spokane and Seattle and Portland, not neglecting to keep sports writers in those cities informed. The doubling and redoubling of publicity had some of the folks back in Shelby wondering what was going on, not least the Shelby chapter of the American Legion. Johnson was chairman of the American Legion Boxing Committee in Shelby, and was acting in that capacity as the pretend promoter of the title fight. The Legionnaires were totally in the dark about what Johnson was up to, and while he was gone they voted him out of his position as chairman of the Boxing Committee.

This action by the Legion would have caused bad publicity if it had gone public, so Johnson hurried back to Shelby and scheduled a night meeting with the Legion to explain himself. By this time newsmen from the outside world were moving in and out of Shelby looking for news about the fight. In his book, Johnson, looking back down the years, wrote that facing his comrades at the Legion, he could not bring himself to admit that the whole thing was a charade. For one thing, the few of his friends who had been in on the joke from the beginning had begun to fall in love with their own publicity, besides which the citizens of Shelby had got all excited about the prospects. Reading between the lines, one gets the feeling that Body Johnson was pretty excited too.

So, the decision was made to actually try to put on the fight. The fight was to be sponsored by the American Legion Boxing Club of Toole Post No. 52, which was incorporated especially for the purpose. A fellow named Loy Molumby, a Great Falls attorney who was State Chairman of the American Legion, was named manager of the boxing club. An uproar immediately ensued because Dempsey had got a lot of bad publicity as a purported draft dodger, having avoided participation in World War I. Nevertheless, things proceeded.

The Shelby crowd soon found out that it was over its head in dealing with the national prizefighting element. Johnson wrote, "No one could have been more ignorant in dealing with fight promoters, managers, and their hangers-on than I was, unless possibly it could have been Loy Molumby." This became significant when events transpired to place Molumby as the sole Montana representative at the contract signing in Chicago.

When the contract was signed, the promoters back in Montana were amused by the newspaper stories saying that it had been agreed to pay Dempsey $300,000, of which $100,000 was to be paid upon signing the contract, a second $100,000 on June 15, and the final payment on July 2, two days before the fight. The folks back in Shelby knew the stories had to be wrong, because they had never considered paying Dempsey more than

$200,000. They were more than slightly surprised when Molumby returned and said sheepishly that he had signed a contract for $300,000. Molumby explained that Dempsey wouldn't fight for less. There were reports that Molumby had been entertained at a big blowout in the hotel before the contract was signed, and Johnson said he didn't think Molumby knew what he was agreeing to when he signed it.

The first $100,000 was raised by ticket subscriptions, and this money was turned over to Dempsey when the contract was signed. Where the remainder was going to come from was problematical. Chaos soon arose. The contract was signed on May 4, and many things had to be done before the fight on July fourth. For example, an arena had to be built from scratch. This construction required a substantial amount of lumber, which ultimately turned out to be 1,000,300 board feet, at a price of $82,000.

The lumbermen in Kalispell would not deliver unless they knew they were going to get paid. It was clear that the fight promoters needed some financial stability. This was provided by Body Johnson's father, James A. Johnson, who reluctantly agreed to become treasurer, which meant that he paid out his own cash when bills came due, hoping that the books could be straightened out later.

Johnson anted up the $82,000 for construction of the stadium, which began on May 19. Upwards of 200 carpenters were on the job, and the arena was completed on June 20. This was a substantial achievement, considering that the stadium covered 6 acres, had 85 rows of seats, and was designed to hold 40,208 persons. With an eye to economy, no backs were put on the seats, to avoid damaging the lumber which was to be resold for use in the oil fields after the stadium was dismantled.

In the weeks that led up to the fight, Shelby became a busy place. Besides the press, all manner of fast and slow buck artists turned up. There was no shortage of sideshows, girly shows, and even rodeos. There were reports in newspapers around the state that vice was running wild in Shelby, with gambling and the swilling of liquor being commonplace. The state's Attorney General, Wellington D. Rankin, took a dim view of this reported activity and threatened to cancel the fight. He said, "Shelby shall not be the rendezvous of thugs, yeggs, plug-uglies, pickpockets, gamblers, rum-runners, or any other class of anarchists who make a living by defying the law and the Constitution." Rankin then visited Shelby, and concluded that the anarchy there had been exaggerated. Reporters from the Great Falls *Tribune* were unable to find anything worse than "the horrible bray of the local jazz bands." A photograph in Johnson's book shows a federal prohibition officer who is said to be "well-pleased over Shelby's drouth." Another source said Shelby's saloons had at least taken their signs down in response to Prohibition.

By mid-May, Dempsey was established in a training camp outside Great Falls. Gibbons trained in Shelby, where he was ensconced in a house with his wife and family. The promoters paid the expenses of both fighters.

As the June 15 deadline approached for the second $100,000, the

Shelby boys were wondering where they were going to get it. They decided to take to the air, barnstorming around to the various Legion posts to sell tickets. Body Johnson, Loy Molumby, a pilot and another man obtained the use of an airplane and began flying around the state to sell the tickets. They touched down at Lewistown, Miles City, and Billings with good results, Johnson said, but after a stop at Livingston they hit a downdraft on takeoff and crashed. Johnson was seriously injured, and that ended the airborne assault on the Legion posts.

The second $100,000 was raised by leaning once again on the people of Shelby to buy advance tickets, which produced $35,000, with another $15,000 coming from some businessmen in Great Falls and the balance from the pocket of James Johnson, senior.

Body Johnson explained in his book why his father and the Great Falls businessmen would give Kearns the second payment without extracting some promise from him to cooperate by assuring news people that the fight would occur. The explanation, he said, was "they just couldn't believe that anyone could be the liar that Kearns turned out to be."

Out west, Johnson wrote, men did business on the strength of a handshake. Kearns and his people were not motivated by this ethic. Kearns kept saying that if the final payment were not made, there would be no fight, and this had a severe effect on ticket sales. Johnson said that around June 15, the Shelby promoters had nearly $500,000 in advance sales, and 26 special trains were scheduled to bring people from all over the country. The Great Northern had expanded its depot in Shelby and built 35 miles of siding to accommodate fight-goers. All of these trains were canceled when it looked like there wasn't going to be a fight. On July 2nd, the promoters agreed to turn all of the gate receipts over to Kearns to make up his third $100,000, and then he finally told the press that there would be a fight. This was too late to help ticket sales, of course.

Ringside seats were $50, with the cheaper seats for $33 and $22. On fight day, a crowd showed up and milled around the 16 entrances to the stadium, yelling, "For $10 we'll come in." There are many versions of what happened next. According to a news account in the Shelby *Promoter* newspaper on fight day, 7,966 people were checked in at the gates, but several thousand people crashed the gates and overwhelmed the gatekeepers before the main bout. Johnson said in his book that the ticket sellers and takers stayed at their posts until the main event started and then "suddenly found their presence very much needed around the ring itself, leaving the gates unguarded." He estimated that 12,000 people saw the fight.

The fight itself was hard work on the blazing hot day, and not a classic display of the manly art of boxing. Gibbons was the first man to last 12 rounds against Dempsey, and certainly the first to last 15. The decision rightfully went to Dempsey. Gibbons fought a defensive battle for most of the fight. Some observers wondered if he was affected by the knowledge that he was working for nothing. His share of the purse was supposed to come from gate receipts after Dempsey had his third hundred thousand.

Gibbons could see from the size of the crowd that there wasn't going to be any third hundred thousand.

Body Johnson took righteous issue with the suggestion that Gibbons was working for nothing. Besides his training expenses, Johnson said, Gibbons had a free house for himself and his family during his stay in Shelby. Besides that, he was allowed to sell tickets to people who came into his training camp, and Johnson said bags of cash were collected each day.

Publicity was Gibbons' main harvest. From a largely unknown, slightly over-the-hill fighter, he had become well known. Soon after the fight, he got a 20-week vaudeville contract for $2,500 a week. He had several more fights after 1923, retiring in 1925 after he was knocked out by Gene Tunney. In 1964, four years after his death, he was inducted into the boxing hall of fame.

There was publicity enough for everybody in Shelby. An actress named Patricia Salmon who performed in one of the tent shows was written up fabulously by some of the visiting reporters who didn't have anything else to do, and on the strength of the publicity she got a contract with Ziegfeld's Follies. She was not up to her notices, however, and by 1928 she was discovered seeking new publicity by dancing 130 hours and 40 minutes in a dance marathon in Madison Square Garden. It didn't work, and she passed into oblivion on swollen feet.

At the conclusion of the fight, Kearns took the cash receipts—$54,000 in a black bag—and slipped out under cover of night. He reportedly paid a railroad engineer $500 to hook a caboose to his engine and take him to Great Falls, where he spent the night in the basement of a barber shop. The next day he escaped to Salt Lake City.

Kearns was not the only one in a hurry to get out of town. "Boy," Johnson wrote, "how the people did leave Shelby the night of the fight— the hangers on, the rodeo promoters and performers, the sideshow performers, and of course, all of the very few cash customers. She was a regular ghost town that night and for some time thereafter."

Shelby had generated about as much publicity as one little town on the prairie was ever likely to produce, but it didn't do a thing for the real-estate market. Johnson wrote in his book that his real-estate firm "didn't sell one damn dollar's worth of real estate. No one wanted to buy, but everyone either wanted a concession or a short-term lease. Even our salesmen were starving at the end of the season."

A few days after the fight, the banks began to close. First was the Stanton Trust and Savings Bank in Great Falls. Body Johnson insisted that the Stanton Bank had liquidated "for their own reasons and not for any shortage of funds." However, the First State Bank of Shelby, "in the face of a few withdrawals that could not under any circumstances be called a run," found itself short of cash. It tried to withdraw funds it had on deposit at the Stanton Bank but the latter was closed, so the Shelby bank closed. This led to a run on the First National Bank of Shelby, which soon closed. The first State Bank of Joplin, which was associated with the First State of Shelby, also closed. Johnson claimed these bank closings had nothing to do with the fight, but the legend runs otherwise. So, the answer is four.

Given time, Shelby recovered from the ghostliness that settled over it after the fight. The oil business continued to boom, and the Johnsons made money not only in oil but also in ranching, livestock, and other endeavors. Body Johnson's father, James A. Johnson, Shelby mayor, banker, and chief financial backer of the fight, took the big loss—$164,500—which came out of his pocket and didn't involve any banks, according to Body Johnson.

Over the years following the fight, Tommy Gibbons visited Shelby several times at the invitation of the town, but Dempsey never returned, despite numerous invitations. For that matter, nobody from Shelby visited him either, despite invitations from mutual friends. Johnson wrote that he often walked by Dempsey's restaurant in New York but never went in. The reason he avoided Dempsey, he said, was because of "the adverse and unfair publicity we had received and the abuse we absorbed."

So it was publicity they were after, and they got it, but it wasn't what they thought. In the world of sports, an event with enough publicity, good or bad, eventually becomes a matter of folklore. So it is with the great Shelby fight. For a brief period, Shelby was the most famous town in the country. It is a good story, and is not likely to die. The 1992 publisher of the Shelby *Promoter* newspaper, John F. Kavanagh, nephew of Body Johnson, told me that he recently had heard from two motion picture producers who were considering making a film about the great event. The old publicity mill that started up in 1923 hasn't run down yet.

LAST OF THE NITRO SHOOTERS

When Charlie Stalnaker died of a heart attack at age 87 in 1979, he was the last nitro shooter to go, and one of the few to go quietly. Most of the others went out with a bang and a flash, and left no body to bury.

Nitro shooters made their living by using nitroglycerine, a notoriously sensitive and violent compound, to blast life into sluggish oil wells. One small mistake, or bad luck, and they had a career-ending blast.

Charlie Stalnaker was born in Georgetown, West Virginia on August 26, 1891. He started working as a tool dresser in the West Virginia oil fields in 1914. Presently he drifted west, and met a man named Dana Walters in Wyoming. Walters was a shooter, and suggested that Stalnaker should go into that line of work. There was an opening. "We had a fella get blowed up over here at Shoshoni," Walters said.

On the 22nd of March, 1922, Stalnaker began his career as a shooter. He migrated around the western oil fields, working wherever his services were needed, and touched down at Shelby once or twice. His old acquaintance Dana Walters was in Shelby, and had built a nitroglycerine factory on the Marias River south of town. On one of his stints in Shelby, Stalnaker built a magazine just north of town for storage of nitro.

Stalnaker returned to Shelby later, after Walters blew himself up in the magazine. Another man replaced Walters, and soon blew himself up. Then Stalnaker replaced the man who replaced Walters. In the oilfields around Shelby, they recall that Walters had been using some "dirty" nitro just before he blew up. "Dirty" nitro has not been washed properly. When a container of dirty nitro is opened, it smokes. It doesn't lack for power, but is more unstable than normal nitro.

Someone noticed that a can of Walters' nitro was smoking, and asked him if that were not dangerous. Walters said, "I've shot worse than this." It was a few months later that Walters blew up, but the oilfield people thought his rightful last words were, "I've shot worse than this."

It was suggested that Walters didn't wash his nitro properly because exposure to it gave him fierce headaches. Stalnaker, speaking in a tape-recorded interview, said Walters "Ate a box of aspirin every time we made nitroglycerine, but I don't think it did him much good."

When nitroglycerine gets inside the body, it speeds up heart action. Some heart patients take nitroglycerine pills for this reason. If fumes are inhaled or if the liquid nitro gets absorbed into the skin, it causes a headache of legendary proportion in many people.

Stalnaker described the manufacture of nitro at the factory he inherited from Walters. First, he said, they took 1,500 pounds of mixed nitric and sulfuric acid and put it into a nitrator unit. In the bottom of this vessel were coils through which water from the river would be pumped to cool the reaction, which gives off substantial heat. Then 285 pounds of glycerine would be added to the acid. Nitroglycerine freezes at 40° F., so ethylene glycol was added to make the nitro freeze-proof in cold weather. After the reaction was complete, the nitro was dumped carefully into a water-filled "drowning tank," and then to washing containers. Hot water at about 150 degrees was pumped into the bottom of these containers. Water is much lighter than nitro, so it would float to the top, washing leftover acid out of the nitro as it rose.

This recipe would produce 600 pounds of nitroglycerine, which was transferred into 10-quart copper cans with cork stoppers, for storage or transport.

Stalnaker said he usually made three or four batches at a time, 1,800 or 2,400 pounds. The nitro was stored in a magazine until it was needed. When it was needed, Stalnaker would go to the magazine with his "shooting car"—in the early days usually a Buick or LaSalle, "a big car with soft springs"—and load the nitro into the nitro box that he built into the trunk. This box had a compartments for each individual can, and in later years was equipped with rubber liners to prevent cans from leaking into a fatal place.

In the early days when shooters traveled in spring wagons, the nitro box was lined with carpet and had straw in the bottom. It was theorized that nitro leaking out of the box and getting on the springs might have been the cause of some blowups. One of the things nitro will not stand for is being compressed, as would happen between spring leaves when the spring flexes. No witness ever explains what caused an accidental nitro explosion, because they are not around afterwards. Stalnaker said he never used a wagon, except once when the roads got so bad a car couldn't get around.

After he had the nitro loaded in his shooting car, Stalnaker would proceed to the well. Sometimes it was near Shelby, and sometimes it was hundreds of miles away. "Old Charlie traveled all over the country with a load of nitro in his car," said Dan Mitchell, a driller who knew Stalnaker for many years.

At the well, the well operator would determine how much nitro was to be used, usually 20 or 30 quarts. "Mostly it was a matter of looking at what worked at a neighboring well, and doing the same thing," Mitchell said. The idea was to fracture the oil-bearing rock formation and release the oil. This process is called "secondary recovery." Today there are many different methods of such recovery, but originally, and when Stalnaker started out, explosives were the only method used.

The nitro was loaded into a "shell," which was made of tin stove-pipes soldered to the right length. The shell was first filled with water, and then the heavier nitro was poured in the top. It would sink gently to the bottom of the shell and displace the water. This avoided the need to pour the nitro from the top to the bottom of the can without any cushioning. "You didn't want to pour glycerine more than about four inches," said Henry Sieben, retired oil man.

When the shell was filled, it was lowered into the well on a quarter-inch manila line, going down to the "pay zone" in the rock, usually at the bottom. This was below the well casing. In later years, the explosive was detonated with a time bomb. The delay provided by the time bomb was necessary because a cement plug was set in the well above the explosive, and a few hours were needed for the cement to harden.

The time bombs had two timepieces—"just a couple of cheap wind-up watches," Mitchell said. Two watches were used rather than rely on a single watch that might stop. The watches were set, and the first watch to reach the set time tripped a mechanical device that fired four .38 cartridges. Bullets from these cartridges went into a quarter stick of dynamite, detonating it, and in turn detonating the nitro.

Before time bombs came on the scene, a "jack squib" was used to detonate the nitro. A jack squib was a piece of pipe similar to a stove pipe, about 4 feet long. A quarter stick of dynamite with fuse was placed on the bottom of the squib, which was then filled with dirt or sand to contain the blast. The fuse was lighted and the squib lowered into the well until it rested on top of the nitro container.

Solidified nitroglycerine, called SNG, came on the scene in the 1920s and was much safer, but a lot of well owners thought it wasn't powerful enough. "Besides," Mitchell said, "Charlie could make a lot more off a shot if he made the nitro himself. If he used the solidified, he had to buy it from DuPont." The nitro factory on the Marias apparently was the only one that ever existed in Montana. There was one in Wyoming, but Dana Walters' brother blew it up, along with himself.

Being blown up was an occupational hazard that could occur anyplace. Sometimes shooters blew up in the nitro factory. Sometimes they blew up in a bunker. Sometimes they blew up on the road. One of the most thorough blowups Stalnaker remembered was "old Homer Russell," in Texas. Homer went up with 3,000 quarts of nitro, 1,300 pounds of solidified nitro, and a ton of dynamite. All they found of Homer was a piece of bone about an inch by an inch and a half. They thought it might have come from a shoulder blade.

Stalnaker said he personally replaced five men who had blown up. In his early days as a shooter, he said, he had worked with 17 other shooters, and he was the last of them still alive. Based on his conversations with Stalnaker, Dan Mitchell said he didn't think very many of the other 17 died quietly.

One of Stalnaker's adventures was flying to Canada to shoot a well in winter when all the roads were blocked. The man with the well sent a pilot to get him in a Stinson airplane, which he landed by the magazine outside of Shelby. There they loaded 100 quarts of nitro. They had a strong head wind all the way, and the pilot was strangely silent. He asked Stalnaker how long it would take to throw out all the nitro in case of engine trouble. "Ten seconds," Stalnaker said, "but farmers are going to think the war has started again when those cans hit the ground." They flew directly over the middle of Calgary and landed at an airfield north of town. After it was on the ground, the plane taxied about 20 feet and ran out of gas. "Next time we refueled at Lethbridge," Stalnaker said.

Stalnaker attributed his long life in his profession to extreme care, and to abstaining from alcohol on the job. "He said the other guys lost their nerve, started drinking, and blew themselves up," Dan Mitchell said. Of course, when Stalnaker wasn't working, he liked to drink about a quart of whiskey a day, one of his acquaintances told me. "Oh yeah, he liked to raise hell, chase women and all that," Mitchell said.

Along with his adventurous life, Stalnaker had time for ordinary pursuits too. He was for a time treasurer of Toole County, for example. He was the father of three children, and outlived two wives.

From Stalnaker's first shooting job in 1922 to his last in 1975 was 53 years. Nowadays, Mitchell said, shooting is not a dangerous job. He said modern explosive comes in big rolls and looks like sausage. It doesn't go off until it is supposed to. Nobody uses homemade nitro anymore.

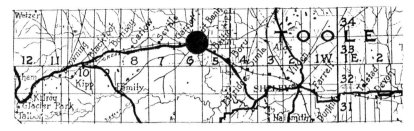

CUT BANK

The Great Northern Railway reached Cut Bank in 1890. This was cattle country then, and the facilities of the town reflected the needs of the cowpunchers' lonely life. A visitor in 1902 inventoried the businesses: eight saloons, a two-story bordello, two stores, two livery barns, two cafes, a blacksmith shop, a rooming house, the Great Northern Hotel, 25 residences and some shacks. Population of the town was said to be about 250.

School began in 1902, with classes held in an abandoned saloon. The same one-room building also served as a funeral home. The building had a stage on one side which was used for the funeral business. When business was at hand in the funeral parlor, the curtain was drawn on the stage.

Homesteaders came in a big way, and by 1912 most of the tillable land was fenced and farmed. Homesteaders did well at first, and the railroad expanded its facilities in Cut Bank to a point where many railroad jobs were created. These were boom times in Cut Bank. The town was incorporated on March 11, 1911.

Glacier County was busted out of Teton County in 1919, and Cut Bank set out to become the county seat. There followed a spirited battle with Browning, which was more nearly in the center of the county and also wanted to be the county seat. The balloting was held in a ranch house five miles west of Cut Bank. The house had a living room 35x60 feet, which wasn't any too big. Witnesses said at least 200 persons were present at all times during the day. A band from Browning came over to lighten up the proceedings, and dancing went on through the night and into the next morning. Indians had not yet received voting rights. If the Indians could have voted, Browning probably would have been the county seat.

With the county seat firmly established, Cut Bank was ready for its next boom. This came in the early 1930s with the discovery of oil in the Cut Bank Field. Some wells in this field were within the town. Cut Bank became an oil town. It is said that the Great Depression passed by Cut Bank, where people were kept prosperous by work associated with oil and gas.

Today, a variety of businesses that provide oil-field services still exist in Cut Bank, but most of them are either closed or having a tough time of it. With time and declining oil prices, the contribution of oil and gas to the local economy has dropped off.

Leanne Kavanagh, editor of the Cut Bank *Pioneer Press,* said losses in the oil and gas business have caused a drop in the county's taxable valuation. Despite these losses, life in the town has many benefits and pleasures, according to Kavanagh. She said the town will continue to enjoy commercial traffic from the Blackfeet Reservation, which begins on the west edge of town, and from Canadians, many of whom are lured down to shop by fliers sent through the mail. Cut Bank has one of the two bona fide shopping malls on the Hi-Line, and this attracts shoppers from far away.

Besides, Kavanagh points out, economics are not everything. "We may be the coldest spot in the nation, but we have the warmest people." The county has fine schools, she said, and these are a point of pride.

The Glacier County Museum north of town has many fine displays, including artifacts from bygone days in the oil field. Among the displays is an original Standard Oil drill rig which drilled many oil and gas wells in the vicinity until the technology was replaced by rotary drilling.

Visitors may wonder about the penguin motif that is seen here and there. Trash cans on the downtown street are in the form of penguins. On the east edge of town, a tourist information facility features a "27-foot talking penguin." This is a way of making light of those numerous days each winter when Cut Bank is the coldest spot in the lower 48.

OIL AND GAS ON THE HI-LINE

There is no doubt that oil and gas development has played an important role in Montana, and particularly on the Hi-Line. Material published by the Montana Geological Society indicates Montana has no fewer than 256 oil and gas fields. Many of these are small or played out, but others still produce well, and could produce more if the incentive were there.

No one has yet produced a comprehensive history of oil and gas in Montana for the layman, but some information is available. Dan Whetstone, long-time newspaper publisher in Cut Bank, once wrote about the typical stages of scouting for oil.

First it is some halfwitted near-geologist or some daydreaming doodlebugger prowling about the prairies and confiding his vision to a homesteader, a sheepherder or the editor of a weekly newspaper, who prints it on a dull week. Then a government geologist comes along and casts a coldly scientific eye over the terrain, examines the escarpments, goes around in great circles to determine whether there is a completed closure. Cautiously he reports in a bulletin or tract that there are some symptoms of a dome. Then a canny or crazy lease hound comes along, blocks up a big tract, peddles it to a wildcatter and the wildcatter goes out and begs or borrows until he has raised enough to make a test.

The record shows that the first oil on the Hi-Line was found in 1904, in what is now Glacier National Park. That first Hi-Line well, which is now under Lake Sherburne, struck a small amount of oil at 387 feet. A subsequent well, also under Lake Sherburne, found a larger quantity of oil at 1,500 feet, with a drilling cost of $19,923. Neither these wells nor two others drilled in the vicinity were commercial producers, but they reportedly produced enough to keep all the farm machinery oiled for miles around and years afterward.

The present author knew nothing about oil drilling, but at least I knew that I knew nothing. To improve myself, I went a few miles north of Shelby to Kevin, an oil town that time seems to have ignored for about 60 years. There I met Conrad Huso, who is universally known as Connie, and who has been in the oil fields man and boy for over 40 years. His father was an oil man and bought land and drilled for oil near Ferdig in 1925. Connie came to Ferdig in 1928 at the age of one-and-a-half. Today he lives in Kevin where he operates The Adicizers, a business that pumps acid into feeble oil wells to improve production.

"These wells around here are in limestone," he said. "You put the acid down to dissolve the limestone and free the oil." He said business has been poor, with only about five wells treated each month. "That's about two thousand or three thousand dollars worth of business," he explained.

The wells in the Kevin-Sunburst Field are between 1,400 and 1,800 feet deep. An acid treatment consists of pumping 200 to 500 gallons of 15 to 30 percent hydrochloric acid solution down the well. It reacts with the limestone, creating carbon dioxide and water. "This field has been going since 1922 and it's pretty well drilled out," he said. "Some wells have been treated 100 times or more."

Having filled me in on acid treatments, Connie made a couple of phone calls and then we went to his office. Presently we were joined by some professors of oilfield lore, whom Connie had summoned on the phone. At least a couple of the professors seemed to have migrated from the direction of the Derrick Bar. Connie explained to me that since it was a rainy day and the roads were all muddy, it was hard to get out to the wells and a lot of the oil people were hanging around waiting for drier weather.

The main professors, besides Connie, were Henry Sieben, retired oil man, Dan Mitchell, who runs his own drilling company, and Marian Irgens, daughter of a local oil man, and authority on most matters having to do with oil. Ms. Irgens runs Connie's office.

Mr. Sieben, who said he damn sure was not related to the sheep-raising Siebens, came to Kevin from Butte in 1934. He held a wide variety of jobs, became an "all-around hand," and "wound up with a little production of my own." Which he used to drill dry holes, according to him.

He said drilling was always interesting. I asked him what was interesting about it. He was stumped for a moment. Ms. Irgens reminded him, "It must have been interesting when the oil blew out."

"Oh yeah," he said.

I asked him if it didn't bother him to lose all the oil that blew out in a gusher.

"Wasn't worth anything anyway," he said. "Maybe two dollars and fifty cents a barrel. There was just a gas bubble in there and it didn't blow very long."

Part of my education was learning what a "Standard Rig" is. That's short for "Standard Oil Rig." Why it's called that I couldn't find out. A Standard Rig is the derrick that you see pictures of and think of as an oil well. These days, drill rigs are truck mounted and don't look much like a Standard Rig. Standard Rigs made of wood were used from the early days of oil drilling. They were nailed together with ordinary lumber, and usually took about four days to assemble. If a well turned out to be a producer, the rig was left in place for use in hoisting tools, pipe, and such.

The steel Standard Rigs were bolted together, and were taken down after a well was completed. The last Standard Rig that anybody knows of around here is in the museum at Cut Bank.

The Standard Rig used a cable tool, which was just a mechanism that lifted a large steel bit at the end of a cable and then let it drop, lifted it and let it drop. The bit that was used to start the hole was sometimes as large as 15½ inches in diameter. As different depths were reached, smaller bits were used, down to 12½, 10¾, 8⅝, 7, 6¼. Cable tools in suitable ground could reach depths of about 5,000 feet.

Standard Rigs were manned by two men, the driller and the tool dresser. The tool dresser's job was to take the worn bits to the forge house next to the rig, heat and resharpen them. In the days when Henry Sieben was becoming an all-around hand in the oil field, the rig men worked 12-hour shifts. A shift in the oil field is called a "tour." In the oilfield, that's pronounced "tower." Only a greenhorn would say "toor." Tours went to eight hours around 1946.

One of the well-known characters in the Kevin-Sunburst field was the future governor of Montana, J. Hugo Aronson, called the "Galloping Swede" from the way he loped around on the job. He is fondly remembered for having once rented a grocery store counter to sleep on in Ferdig.

Dan Mitchell, another professor, started working in the oil field when he was 14 years old. "That was fifty years ago," he said. During World War II, he said, so many men were gone to the military that kids were recruited to work the oil fields. "Kids would get out of school at three o'clock, and work on a rig from four to midnight."

Mitchell eventually went to Gonzaga University, where he got a degree in mechanical engineering, and then returned to his previous haunts. "I guess I'm just oil patch trash," he said. Today he runs Comanche Drilling

Company, located in Cut Bank.

For the first 15 years or so that Mitchell was working in the oil business, all the rigs were Standard Rigs. Then, about 1956, rotary drills came on the scene. Rotary drills are much more complicated than Standard Rigs. A bit with three toothed wheels is rotated at the end of a shaft. A drilling medium, usually called "mud," is pumped down the well and through ports in the bit. This mud lubricates and cools the bit. Mud is continuously pumped into the well, and after it comes out the ports in the bit it is forced back to the surface, carrying the cuttings with it. The actual composition of the mud is widely varied to meet different conditions. Common variations include weight, consistency, and acidity. For shallow wells, less than 3,000 feet, compressed air is sometimes used as the drilling medium. Rotary rigs can go down to 15,000 feet with one size pipe, unlike the Standard Rig.

Four men are needed to run a rotary rig: the driller, the derrick man, the motor man, and the floor man. These four all work for the tool pusher, who is the boss of the rig. The driller bosses the three men below him, the derrick man bosses the motor man and the floor man, the derrick man bosses the floor man, and the floor man takes his lumps.

Mitchell enlarged upon Henry Sieben's statement that drilling is always an interesting job. "For one thing, it's fun because it's a gamble. You never know what you'll get. And on the rig, it seems like something happens every day. Maybe the crew shows up drunk. Maybe you lose something down the hole and have to do a fishing job. Or maybe [back on a Standard Rig] the driller was dumb, and I mean real dumb, and he didn't notice that the tool string had come apart and he drilled on it all night, thinking the hole had got hard. When that happens, part of the tool string pounding all night on the other part, you have a mushroom head. Sometimes it would mushroom to the point where you couldn't get it out of the hole without filing it down. We'd send down a rasp that would file enough of the mushroom off so we could send a fishing tool down to pull it up. Then we'd have to put it on a truck to take to the welding shop to fix, and people would see it and say, 'Who's the dummy?'"

Business is not great these days, but Mitchell said he had a contract to drill four holes.

In a later telephone conversation, Mitchell reflected on the changing technology of oil drilling. "Looking out my window here [Cut Bank] toward the airport, I can see them drilling a horizontal well. They go down until they hit the pay zone, and they just turn ninety degrees and drill horizontally. And they know where the bit is all the time."

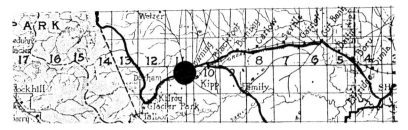

BROWNING

It seems clear that there is a town called Browning in Glacier County, but details of its history are difficult to pin down. The Montana Historical Society does not have a file on Browning, although virtually every wide spot in the road is represented there.

From sketchy information, it appears that the site of Browning was selected as the location of the Blackfeet Agency in 1895, as the government completed yet another shrinkage of the Blackfeet Reservation. Apparently named after D.M. Browning, Commissioner of Indian Affairs at the time, the town of Browning was incorporated in 1918 or 1919, and gave good account of itself in a struggle with Cut Bank in an effort to become county seat for the newly created Glacier County.

Browning is the home of the Blackfeet Indians and headquarters for tribal government. The town is well-known as the location of the Museum of the Plains Indian, and the studio of sculptor Bob Scriver. Located on Highway 2, the town is passed through by thousands of tourists on their way to Glacier Park. Economic planners for the Tribe are considering various ways of tapping the tourist potential of the reservation. The town has modern motels (though not enough, according to the planners), stores, and is home to the Blackfeet Community College. The Blackfeet planners have many ideas about development in the town and elsewhere on the reservation.

The Blackfeet Planning Office is located in a little pink house in Browning. In a room at one end, Stu Miller, head of the office, sits at a computer terminal. He is working on a grant proposal. The deadline for applications is the next day; it is almost the worst time possible for a drifter to come in and ask questions. But there I am, and he generously takes time to fill me in on his work.

"Planning on the reservation is guided by concern for tribal culture, the environment, and the needs of the people," he said. "We consider protection of the environment to be particularly important. We actively pursue programs to protect the quality of our air and water." Miller said planning on the reservation takes a "multi-media approach." On the reservation, "multi-media" means earth, air and water, he said.

One current prospect for economic development is the potential development of wind-powered electrical generation. Miller said the Blackfeet Reservation has 85 percent of the potential wind energy in the entire Northwest. "There is strong interest by developers, but we haven't identified a market that would pay the rate necessary," he said.

Another possible development is gambling. The reservation had limited gambling for a time, but this was shut down pending conclusion of a compact with the state. The Tribe proposed a compact, and was negotiating with state government. Presumably, gambling will return at some point.

"Like the other tribes," Miller said, "we have been approached by outside developers who would like to build a casino on the reservation. They want to build in East Glacier." At such time as a compact is completed, Miller said, the tribe may take a look at allowing a casino on the reservation, but will take a go-slow approach. "Right now, the water and sewage systems are not up to handling a casino," he said. "All these things have to be planned for. We want tourism and growth, but we want growth from within. We don't want an influx of outsiders."

One strong point in the reservation economy has been the development of commercial campgrounds on the reservation. "We have two KOA campgrounds. These have been profitable, and have created jobs."

Oil and gas development remains a force in the economics of the reservation, Miller said, with 570 "more or less producing wells." There is potential for additional development, Miller said, noting that the tribe's Oil and Gas Department has been reorganized and beefed up with additional staff to investigate the potential.

Sport fishing is one of the main reasons many people visit the reservation, Miller said. He said the tribe's management of the fisheries has created fishing that brings people from all over the world. No state fishing license is required on the reservation. A tribal fishing permit costs $30 for the season, or $20 for three days, or $7.50 for one day. As we talked about fishing, Miller showed me snapshots of his family with ridiculously large trout they have caught. "I've been catching them ever since I was a boy," he says. He tells me his secret bait. If I wrote it here, it wouldn't be a secret anymore.

For further information, Miller suggested I talk to Feral Wagner, a planner for the Economic Development Administration, with her office in the same pink building.

Ms. Wagner speaks softly, but she is frustrated. It seems that the forces on the other side of the mountains have hogged all the publicity for Glacier National Park, and have even pirated some of the resources on the east side for themselves.

"All the advertising you see always excludes Glacier County," she said. To hear the Westsiders from the Flathead tell it, the Glacier Park road ends at St. Mary Lake, she said. They even claim the east side's scenery, publicizing their offerings with photographs of St. Mary Lake with Goose Island. That's the big lake with the little island that makes it onto all road maps and Glacier Park publicity materials. It is permanently located at the east side of the park. Ms. Wagner said she will continue to agitate for better recognition for the east side.

In the meantime, Wagner said, new projects are underway to take advantage of the scenic and recreational resources on the reservation. These projects include horseback rides, wagon rides, and cross-country skiing. She said the community lacks some of the facilities it needs to become a year-round attraction. For example, Browning has three motels, but two of them are closed nine months a year. This limits places to stay for winter visitors.

"We need to build up Browning rather than send people to Cut Bank and East Glacier," she said. Part of the job of building up the town will fall to the Chamber of Commerce, which has only recently come into being. Wagner said that among other chores the Chamber would clean up the town and make it a more desirable place to visit.

In the meantime she said, the tribe is making inquiries about adding motels to the town, and has long-range plans to promote fishing on the reservation. Also, the Tribe is considering updating its campgrounds, to bring them up to the competition in the surrounding area.

Other economic development on the reservation relates to interpretation of the Blackfeet culture for non-Indians. To learn about this, I talked to Curly Bear Wagner, in the adjoining office.

Curly Bear Wagner is Cultural Coordinator for the Blackfeet. He is a large, quiet man with a dry sense of humor. I came into his office and begin rattling off questions about possible schemes to improve life for the Blackfeet. He remained quiet for a few moments, considering. Then he said quietly, "This the 500th anniversary of Columbus huh? Maybe we'll put everybody back on the boat." A few minutes later he said, "Maybe we'll cut our suspenders and go straight up."

In a more serious mood, he talked about the recent accomplishments of the tribe. He said that the tribe recently got a psychological boost when it recovered the remains of some of its ancestors from the Field Museum in Chicago and the Smithsonian Institution in Washington, D.C.

As far as economic opportunities for the tribe, Wagner said more Blackfeet need to get into arts and crafts. "The talent is out there," he said. "It needs to be motivated. There's big money for native peoples." Besides providing a few bucks for the artists, Wagner said participation in the arts would have social benefits. "Right now, when somebody comes out of detox, there's nothing for them to do. Art would help them get going again," he said.

Doing his part for cultural values and economic development, Wagner gives tours of historic cultural sites on the reservation. He offers half-day and full-day options. The half-day trip costs $50 for adults and visits 21 sites. The full-day tour goes to 36 sites for $100. Wagner said the tour is an effort to share the culture, tradition, and history of the Blackfeet with others.

We went on to talk about other aspects of Blackfeet culture, such as the sweat ceremony, performed with a sweat lodge. "In the Indian tradition," he said, "when somebody invites you to a sweat, you give 'em whatever you think, maybe a piece of meat or some money. If somebody says, 'I'm giving a sweat, and you can come for $500,' they are phony."

Are there many phonies? He handed me a list of phonies, which includes some New Age types who make money by holding counterfeit Indian ceremonies. Wagner told me what happened when he showed up at one of them, and we laughed. "They were surprised to see a real Indian there," he said.

I asked him what is the difference between the philosophy of white men and that of the Indians.

"White men came over here through Ellis Island. When they came through there, they left their culture behind. In place of their culture from then on they had the Constitution and the Bill of Rights. From then on, an idea was their whole way of life.

"For us, we had been here thousands of years and put down our roots. We developed an understanding of what the country was about. The white man is like a tourist who only passes through, or a hawk that goes here and there but never stays, is never satisfied. He'll say, 'Let's go over here and explore for oil [gesturing to the right] and then we'll go over there [gesturing to the left] and screw that up.' Look at the environment and you can see the results of this.

"I had a guy from Cleveland tell me, 'Well, it's too bad we had to take your land and put you on a reservation, but you were in the way of progress.' I said to him, 'Oh yeah, Cleveland—that's where the river catches on fire. You're sure right that no Indian would have thought of that.'

"Now," Wagner said, "white people are learning the wisdom of the Indian way of life. We stick together and help each other. We are survivors. We can take anything they throw at us." He said the missions and the Bureau of Indian Affairs tried to destroy their culture, but it survived anyway. In 1979 Congress passed the Indian Religious Freedom Act, which allowed Indians to practice their traditional religion. These days, Wagner said, Blackfeet kids learn their culture in the schools, which do a good job of teaching it.

"Indians have always been great socializers," Wagner said. He pointed to the popularity of powwows, which he said are a continuation of the old-time socializing.

The white man's contribution to Indian socializing has been one of the great problems for the tribes, he said. "Indians socialized with the pipe. White men socialize with the bottle. When Indians began socializing in the white man's way, it was bad for us."

Wagner said that if Europeans had not come to America, Indian culture sooner or later would have been influenced by the Mayas of Central America. He noted that the Maya were an advanced civilization, more advanced than the Europeans. "We would have been people that understood each other. We would have kept the buffalo. We weren't in that big a hurry."

Wagner said greater understanding is needed between Indians

and whites. "Come up and see us," he said. "Don't be strangers." He recommended his tour as a good way to get acquainted. He said that books and articles about the Blackfeet are misleading. "What you read are stereotypes," he said. "Anthropologists are wrong about us sixty percent of the time."

For his closing note, Wagner said that everybody should remember that all people came originally from Adam and Eve.

Anyone interested in Mr. Wagner's tour can call him at 338-2058.

THE BLACKFEET WRITING COMPANY

Purchasers of pens and pencils may note that some of them are made by the Blackfeet Writing Company, a pen and pencil factory owned by the Blackfeet Tribe. The Blackfeet Writing Company is located in a large building in the Browning Industrial Park, outside town. Founded in 1971, the Company produces wooden pencils in round and hexagonal form, along with five different types of ballpoint pens and five different types of felt-tip markers. The company also makes Lindy pens.

Plant manager Marty Meineke said the products from the factory are trucked from Browning to Great Falls, and from there to various destinations. One big market is the Fortune 500 companies, Meineke said. Sales and marketing for the company are handled out of New Jersey. Meineke said 12 salesmen headquartered in New Jersey cover the whole country. "They basically go around knocking on doors," Meineke said. Products from the factory also are sold through Kmart and two mail-order houses, Coldwater Creek and Rivertown.

Meineke said business took a downturn in 1990 and 1991, right along with other business all over the country. "Our big orders haven't been quite as big," he said.

The Writing Company provides much-needed employment on the reservation, with 26 jobs that pay an average of $5.25 an hour. Payroll is about $8,000 a week. Job openings are not frequent. "Everybody here has been here at least four years," Meineke said.

The most popular product from the factory, Meineke said, is the Blackfeet Indian Pencil No. 2. The most popular pen is the Blackfeet Indian Pen in black.

Population Figures and Percentages of Change
Montana Hi-Line Counties, 1900-1990

(figure in parentheses shows percentage of change from previous census)

County (year of creation)	1900	1910	1920	1930	1940	1950	1960	1970	1980	1990
Blaine (1912)			9,057	9,006 (-0.6)	9,566 (+6.2)	8,516 (-11.0)	8,091 (-5.0)	6,727 (-16.9)	6,999 (+4.0)	6,728 (-3.9)
Glacier (1919)			4,178	5,297 (+26.8)	9,034 (+70.5)	9,645 (+6.8)	11,565 (+19.9)	10,783 (-6.8)	10,628 (-1.4)	12,121 (+14.0)
Hill (1912)			13,958	13,775 (-1.3)	13,304 (-3.4)	14,285 (+7.4)	18,653 (+30.6)	17,358 (-6.9)	17,985 (+3.6)	17,654 (-1.8)
Liberty (1920)			2,416	2,198 (-9.0)	2,209 (+0.5)	2,180 (-1.3)	2,624 (+20.4)	2,359 (-10.1)	2,329 (-1.3)	2,295 (-1.5)
Phillips (1915)			9,311	8,208 (-11.8)	7,892 (-3.8)	6,334 (-19.7)	6,027 (-4.9)	5,386 (-10.6)	5,367 (-0.4)	5,163 (-3.8)
Roosevelt (1919)			10,347	10,672 (+3.1)	9,806 (-8.1)	9,580 (-2.3)	11,731 (+22.5)	10,365 (-11.5)	10,467 (+1.0)	10,999 (+5.1)
Toole (1914)			3,724	6,714 (+80.3)	6,769 (+0.8)	6,867 (+1.4)	7,904 (+15.1)	5,839 (-26.1)	5,559 (-4.8)	5,046 (-9.2)
Valley (1893)	4,355	13,630 (+213.0)	11,542 (-15.3)	11,181 (-3.1)	15,181 (+35.8)	11,353 (-25.2)	17,080 (+50.4)	11,471 (-32.8)	10,250 -10.6	8,239 (-19.6)

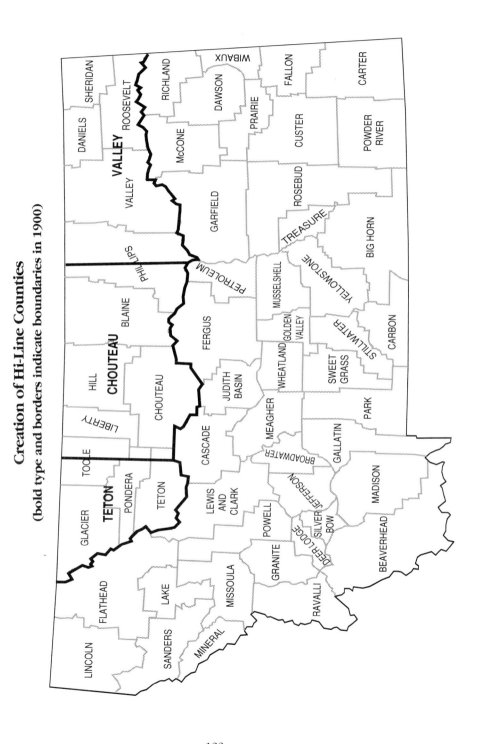

Creation of Hi-Line Counties
(bold type and borders indicate boundaries in 1900)

FOR FURTHER READING

I have relied heavily on the files of the Montana Historical Society Library for historical information. Where no other source is listed below, all information was from the Historical Society. Other sources are listed below for each topic.

The Dempsey-Gibbons Fight
The Fight that Won't Stay Dead, Body Johnson; Promoter Publishing Company, Shelby, Montana, May 23, 1989.
White Hopes and Other Tigers, John Lardner; J.B. Lippincott Company, New York. 1947.
"Shelby's Fabled Day in the Sun," Tony Dalich, *Montana: The Magazine of Western History*, July, 1965.

The History and Construction of Highway 2
"The Historic Development of Montana's Road and Trail System," Marilyn Wyss, Archaeologist, Montana Department of Transportation, Helena. 1992.
Roosevelt County's Treasured Years, Leota Hoye, Poplar, Editor. 1976.

The History of Plentywood and Scobey
Sheridan's Daybreak, Magnus Aasheim, Editor. 1970.
Daniels County History, by the Daniels County Bicentennial Committee, 1977.
"Radical Rule in Montana," Charles Vindex, *Montana: The Magazine of Western History*, Winter, 1968.

Fort Peck Dam
Fort Peck—A Half Century and Still Holding, 50th Anniversary Commemorative Issue, "The District News." Public Affairs Office, Omaha District, U.S. Army Corps of Engineers. Summer, 1987.
Fort Peck, A Job Well Done, October 1933, August 1977. Fort Peck Reunion and Rededication Committee, No date.
Glasgow Courier, Fortieth Anniversary Fort Peck Commemorative Edition. August 1-7, 1977.

History of Shelby
Shelby Backgrounds, Shelby History Group, Montana Institute of the Arts. 1964.

History of Havre
Grit, Guts and Gusto, A History of Hill County, Hill County Bicentennial Commission, Signe M. Sedlacek, Chairwoman. 1976.
Honky Tonk Town: Havre's Bootlegging Days, Gary A. Wilson. High-Line Books, Havre, Montana. 1985.

INDEX

Daniel N. Vichorek was born in Livingston, Montana. He lived with his parents on various Montana ranches for the first 18 years of his life. He enlisted in the Marine Corps after high school graduation. Following military service, he earned a journalism degree at the University of Montana. He later worked as a news reporter with the Billings Gazette *and the* City News Bureau of Chicago. *In between, he spent five seasons as a mule packer for the National Park Service. Currently, he is employed as a technical editor with the Montana Department of Natural Resources and Conservation where he deals primarily with energy conservation matters. He is the author of* Montana's Homestead Era *and* Montana Farm & Ranch Life *in the Montana Geographic Series and is a frequent contributor to* Montana Magazine.